The Enlightenment: A Very Short Introduction

VERY SHORT INTRODUCTIONS are for anyone wanting a stimulating and accessible way into a new subject. They are written by experts, and have been translated into more than 40 different languages.

The series began in 1995, and now covers a wide variety of topics in every discipline. The VSI library now contains over 400 volumes—a Very Short Introduction to everything from Psychology and Philosophy of Science to American History and Relativity—and continues to grow in every subject area.

Very Short Introductions available now:

Available soon:

For more information visit our website

www.oup.com/vsi/

John Robertson

THE ENLIGHTENMENT

A Very Short Introduction

OXFORD
UNIVERSITY PRESS

OXFORD
UNIVERSITY PRESS

Great Clarendon Street, Oxford, OX2 6DP,
United Kingdom

Oxford University Press is a department of the University of Oxford.
It furthers the University's objective of excellence in research, scholarship,
and education by publishing worldwide. Oxford is a registered trade mark of
Oxford University Press in the UK and in certain other countries

© John Robertson 2015

The moral rights of the author have been asserted

First edition published in 2015

Published in the United States of America by Oxford University Press
198 Madison Avenue, New York, NY 10016, United States of America

British Library Cataloguing in Publication Data
Data available

Library of Congress Control Number: 2015935540

ISBN 978-0-19-959178-7

Printed and bound by
CPI Group (UK) Ltd, Croydon, CR0 4YY

For Cleo

Contents

Acknowledgements

I am most grateful to Avi Lifschitz and Brian Young, as well as to two anonymous readers for OUP, for reading the complete draft and making many acute suggestions; likewise to Maxine Berg, Dmitri Levitin and Sarah Mortimer for constructive criticism of individual chapters, which resulted in their considerable improvement. I also owe a great deal to Silvia Sebastiani and her colleagues at the École des Hautes Études en Sciences Sociales, Paris, and to my colleagues and students on the MPhil in Political Thought and Intellectual History at Cambridge, where many of the ideas in this book were tested in discussion. Fo Orbell gave invaluable assistance in identifying the images used as illustrations. Finally, and as ever, I am grateful for the support of my family, to the newest member of which this book is dedicated.

List of illustrations

Chapter 1
The Enlightenment

Few moments in the history of thought have been the subject of so much disagreement as the Enlightenment. As a historical phenomenon, the Enlightenment is identified with an intellectual movement of 18th-century Europe—a movement characterized by certain distinctive ideas, but also by the commitment of its adherents to engaging with a wider public of readers and practitioners. But even in the 18th century, the Enlightenment's significance was believed to transcend its immediate historical circumstances: it held out the prospect of a new, explicitly modern understanding of human beings' place in the world, and of radical improvement in the human condition. Since then what the Enlightenment represents has continued to be the subject of critical discussion, by philosophers as much as by historians, through the 19th and 20th centuries and on into the 21st. Why the Enlightenment 'still matters' is, if anything, more debated now than at any time in the past.

The purpose of this book is to outline what the Enlightenment was in its 18th-century setting, and to explain why it has been so contested since. The key to understanding the Enlightenment, I shall suggest, is to recognize that it was from the beginning associated with 'philosophy', as that term was variously construed in the 18th century. Further, the philosophical ideas of 'Enlightenment' were identified with the 'modern', and, increasingly, with 'modernity' itself. In ways to be explained, therefore, Enlightenment was a philosophical idea before it became a subject for historical investigation. When it did come under historical scrutiny, in the 20th century, the Enlightenment was discovered to have been a broader, more complex movement than had previously been appreciated. But Enlightenment has remained as much a philosophical idea as a historical phenomenon, and because of this, an idea whose meaning and significance have acquired an importance far exceeding other, purely historical occurrences. It is not only scholars and their students who are touched by it, but a much wider public, many of whom bitterly oppose what they believe it to stand for. This book will not disabuse the Enlightenment's enemies, but I hope it may correct some misconceptions, and offer a fresh perspective.

To reconstruct what the Enlightenment was and has become, we must first address the issue of definition, beginning in the 18th century itself.

Contemporary definitions

'Enlightenment' has had many translations. Or rather, the English term Enlightenment is itself a translation, coined in the late 19th century, of two distinct terms, both in use in the 18th century: the French *lumières* and the German *Aufklärung*. The two have in common the idea of 'light'; the French noun, however, is in the plural, while the German indicates less a light shining than a process of enlightenment. Light then carried a strong religious connotation: Christ was the light of the world, a light that we let into our souls. But it also had an older association with philosophy, going back to Plato. Light is knowledge of the true, which we acquire as we leave the caves whose walls of prejudice and ignorance have obscured our vision. This association was reclaimed early in the 18th century by Bernard de Fontenelle (1657–1757), Secretary of the Académie des Sciences in Paris, when he explicitly identified 'lumière' with 'un *esprit philosophique* presque tout nouveau'—a philosophical spirit almost entirely new. By 1751, the association between philosophy and the 'progress' of *lumières* had been enshrined in Jean D'Alembert's 'Discours préliminaire' to the first volume of the great *Encyclopédie, ou dictionnaire raisonné des sciences, des arts et des metiers*, of which D'Alembert (1717–83) was joint editor with Denis Diderot (1713–84).

D'Alembert intended the 'Preliminary Discourse' to provide an intellectual framework for the *Encyclopédie* as a whole. To this end he offered both what he called a 'genealogy' of the human understanding and a historical account of the progress—'les progrès'—of knowledge since the 16th century. By the 'genealogy' of the understanding he meant its genesis in the senses: ideas derive either directly from sensations, or reflectively, through the subsequent combination and comparison of different ideas. This was a truth acknowledged by ancient and even Scholastic philosophy, although it had recently been challenged by the proposition that there are innate ideas. In the domain of nature, our knowledge may be ordered by mathematics, but it ultimately derives from experience. In relation to ourselves, the most important branches of knowledge are those stimulated by the needs of self-preservation. These include study of the languages in which we communicate, of history as the record of experience, and of morals and politics. Only in relation to the arts, including the mechanical arts, were the senses insufficient, meaning that they needed to be supplemented by the imagination (Figure 1).

When he turned to the history of the 'progress' of knowledge, D'Alembert hailed the English philosophers Bacon, Newton, and Locke of the previous century as the modern exponents of this account of understanding as derived from the senses. The error of innate ideas, alas, was associated with the French philosopher, Descartes. In the present century, however, the French had

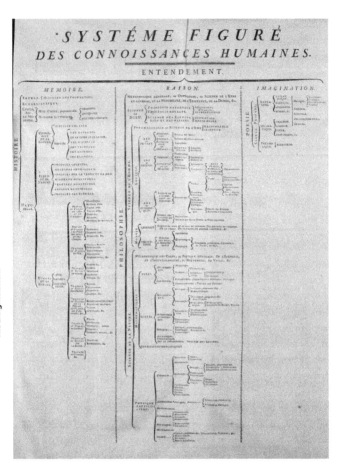

1. The tree of knowledge, from the *Encyclopédie* of D'Alembert and Diderot. The idea of a tree of knowledge, or 'systematic depiction of human knowledge', was not original to the *Encyclopédie*, but it enabled D'Alembert to illustrate his 'genealogy' of the understanding in a graphic form.

repudiated Descartes, and adopted the sense-based philosophy of Locke, whose followers now included Voltaire, Montesquieu, Condillac, and Buffon.

In associating *lumières* with this particular philosophy, D'Alembert aligned Enlightenment explicitly with the cause of the 'moderns' over the 'ancients'. He did this by taking sides in the contemporary debate or *Querelle* between 'ancients and moderns', concerned with the relative merits of the literature and philosophy of ancient Greece and Rome and of modern Europe. D'Alembert's attachment to modern thinking was not exclusive: he acknowledged that ancient philosophy too had derived knowledge from the senses, and that admiration for the ancients had inspired the revival of erudition at the time of the 'renaissance of letters' in the 16th century. But the 'philosophy' of which D'Alembert was the champion was clearly that of the 'moderns'. By the same token, he was connecting that philosophy with what historians call the 'Scientific Revolution' of the 17th century. Now used reluctantly, the term oversimplifies a more complex process of expansion and change in the several branches of what contemporaries called 'natural philosophy'. But D'Alembert was convinced that those recent advances in the understanding of nature had transformed philosophy, and in doing so had reset the foundations of enquiry into human society as well.

The same conclusion had already been reached by two other philosophers, the Abbé Condillac (1714–80) and the Scot, David Hume (1711–76). Both Condillac's *Essai sur l'origine des connoissances humaines* (*Essay on the Origin of Human Knowledge*) (1746) and Hume's *Treatise of Human Nature* (1739–40) were presented by their authors as developing the implications of Locke's argument for the sensory basis of ideas. Condillac made his account of the understanding the basis for a new account of the origin of language and hence of all human culture, while Hume declared his ambition to be no less than the elaboration of a new 'science of man'. Although apparently unaware of Hume's contribution when he wrote the 'Preliminary Discourse', D'Alembert's choice of philosophy to identify with *lumières* accorded with the dominant tendency in contemporary French and British intellectual culture.

Other philosophical systems were of course current at the time, notably the materialism of the Dutch-Jewish philosopher Benedict Spinoza (1632–77) and the rationalism of the German polymath Gottfried Leibniz (1646–1716). According to Spinoza, God and Nature are simply different 'modes' of one 'substance': God is manifest everywhere in nature, and nature is God. God therefore exerts no external, 'providential' power over nature; nature is already always determined in itself. As we shall see in Chapter 2, some historians now wish to draw a close connection between Spinoza's 'monist' metaphysics and a 'radical Enlightenment' whose priority was the critique of religion. By contrast, Leibniz and his follower Christian Wolff (1679–1754) upheld the possibility of a holistic comprehension of the world, in which natural forces and human agents interacted in a harmony ordained by God but accessible to human reason. The possibility of a metaphysics founded on pre-established (*a priori*) first principles would in turn be the starting point of the formulation of a new 'critical' philosophy by Immanuel Kant (1724–1804) in the 1780s (Figure 2).

At that point, moreover, a new association of philosophy with Enlightenment emerged as an alternative to that drawn by D'Alembert. By 1783, use of the German term *Aufklärung* was becoming so frequent that a contributor to the *Berlinische Monatsschrift* sought clarification with a direct question 'Was ist Aufklärung?'—'What is Enlightenment?' Overwhelmingly the responses identified *Aufklärung* with philosophy rather than religion. To Moses Mendelssohn (1729–86), the leading Jewish philosopher of the time, Enlightenment denoted theoretical understanding, and should be regarded as the indispensable handmaid of culture and education.

2. Immanuel Kant (1724–1804), one of the greatest philosophers of the 18th century and indeed of any age, was born, lived, and died in Königsberg, then in East Prussia, now Kaliningrad.

The most famous answer, however, was that of Immanuel Kant. In his essay *Was ist Aufklärung?* (*What is Enlightenment?*) (1784), Kant defined *Aufklärung* as the freedom to make public use of one's reason with the goal of liberating mankind from its self-imposed immaturity. By 'reason', Kant had in mind the philosophy adumbrated in his *Critique of Pure Reason* (1781), where he argued that reason, elaborating *a priori*, categorical propositions of cause and substance, was the prerequisite of our understanding of both the physical and the moral worlds.

In 'What is Enlightenment?' Kant specifically recommended the use of reason in matters of religion, but he clearly intended that it be applied to any subject that could be of benefit to mankind. By the 'public' use of reason, Kant meant its free expression in print; he contrasted this with the 'private' duty of office-holders—public officials, clergy, scholars, and citizens generally—to fulfil the terms of their office. A clergyman, for example, should not question the creed of his church when he preaches, or a professor the requirements of his chair in his lectures; but both should be free to address their fellow-citizens, and their king, on matters of general public concern. Like Mendelssohn, Kant was confident that Prussia's king, Frederick II, understood his message: this, he declared, is 'the age of enlightenment, or the age of Frederick'. But it was not yet an 'enlightened age'; Kant was not so confident of Frederick's successor, the blinkered Frederick William II. The process of enlightenment needed to continue.

The economy and clarity of Kant's answer to the question have made it tempting to let it do duty for a definition of the Enlightenment *tout court*. But this is misleading, for two reasons. First, the philosophy Kant associated with *Aufklärung* was not that of D'Alembert—indeed, Kant's was founded on a systematic critique of the view that understanding derives solely from experience; for their part, the French—and David Hume—were far from sharing Kant's confidence that reason was the key to philosophic understanding. If both *Aufklärung* and *lumières* were identified with 'philosophy', it was not at all the same philosophy. Second, Kant characterized *Aufklärung* as a process, not as a finite phenomenon or period carrying the definite article. A definition of 'the Enlightenment' still lay some distance in the future.

Underlining this point, the earliest uses of Enlightenment in English and *Illuminismo* in Italian, a hundred years or more later, were as translations of the German *Aufklärung*. In both cases, it was idealist philosophers, self-conscious heirs of Kant and Hegel, who coined the translations. Their use of the term, however, was increasingly critical: the philosophy of the Enlightenment belonged to the past, and had been superseded by that of Hegel. By both defining and contesting Enlightenment in these ways, philosophers tightened their grip on the concept, pre-empting its association with other dimensions of thought: religious, literary, and (except at second hand) scientific. Later, in the 20th century, historians would seek to loosen the association with philosophy, and to identify Enlightenment with a much wider range of intellectual activity. But the philosophers' interest in the subject has not diminished—on the contrary, they have continued to claim and contest the Enlightenment ever since, with consequences to which I will return in Chapter 5.

A further, final reinforcement of the identification of 'philosophy' with *lumières* came from the *philosophes'* fiercest critics, the anti-*philosophes* of late 18th-century France. Although they did not make systematic use of the term *lumières*, these critics explicitly identified *philosophie* and its exponents, the *philosophes* or the 'Encyclopedic school', with irreligion and the subversion of the social and political order of the French monarchy. Their attacks had begun as early as the 1760s, escalated sharply in the 1780s, and reached a crescendo in the 1790s, as the events of the Revolution seemed to bear out their worst fears of the pernicious consequences of 'philosophy'.

The most notorious such denunciation was that of the Abbé Barruel, who alleged in 1797 that the Revolution was the direct outcome of an anti-Christian *philosophe* conspiracy. The charge was heard again, with redoubled ferocity, after Napoleon's defeat and the Bourbon Restoration in 1815; and for the next fifty years even liberal historians, such as the great Alexis de Tocqueville, explained the intellectual origins of the Revolution within this framework. Although Tocqueville did not use the language of conspiracy, he believed that the high level of abstraction characteristic of the thinking of the *philosophes* or *gens de lettres* had played a critical part in giving the French people dangerously unrealistic expectations of 'liberty'.

Historical reconstructions

Historical distance entered studies of the Enlightenment only in the early 20th century. French literary historians, led by Gustave Lanson and his pupils Daniel Mornet and Paul Hazard, were the first to apply scholarship to the question of the Revolution's 'intellectual origins', and to set aside the simple-minded equation of *philosophie* and revolution. In the 1930s, younger opponents of fascism, such as the Italian historian Franco Venturi, reopened investigation of the intellectual world of the *Encyclopédie*, and took a much more positive view of Diderot's political radicalism. The new perspective received a fresh boost after World War II, as literary scholars and historians across the Continent sought to offer Europe a better past than the one it had recently experienced. Instead of the nationalism and racial doctrines of the 19th century, they looked back to the now much more attractive 18th century, and found 'the Enlightenment'.

It was in the 1950s and 1960s, therefore, that the Enlightenment at last established itself in the academic and general public's consciousness, and was identified with a broad movement of ideas to which the *philosophes* and their allies elsewhere in Europe had subscribed. It is important to recognize that this was a retrospective 'construction' on the part of scholars. There is nothing inherently wrong with such reconstruction. Historians, including literary scholars and historians of philosophy, must bring their own categories to bear on the past in order to make sense of it. As they are used now, the 'Renaissance', the 'Scientific Revolution', and the 'Enlightenment' are all the constructions of historians. In the case of Enlightenment, the existence of the terms *lumières* and *Aufklärung* in the 18th century has lent credibility to the historians' concept. But the past and present usages are not identical: having once constructed 'the Enlightenment', historians have been free to develop and expand what they mean by it.

As a result, what can be associated with Enlightenment has expanded geographically, socially, and intellectually, well beyond the initial associations of *lumières* and *Aufklärung*. Initially, the geography of Enlightenment seemed simple. *Lumières* radiated outwards from Paris, while *Aufklärung* manifested itself in a handful of German-speaking cities: Berlin, Göttingen, and Königsberg (the city of Kant, now Kaliningrad, a Russian enclave surrounded by Poland and Lithuania). If others were to be associated with either of these expressions of Enlightenment—David Hume, for instance, or the Italians Cesare Beccaria and Ferdinando Galiani—it was as corresponding or visiting members.

The first to challenge these assumptions was Franco Venturi, the greatest of Enlightenment historians, when in 1953 he called upon fellow Italians to focus their attention on their own *Illuminismo*, by identifying and connecting the many within Italy who had taken up the cause of Enlightened reform in the mid and late 18th century. A decade later, the centrifugal tendency in Enlightenment studies was reinforced by the holding of the first International Enlightenment Congress, at Geneva in 1963. Soon the Enlightenment was being discovered in a range of national contexts: in Spain, Scandinavia, Scotland, Eastern Europe, and the North American Colonies. For a while, it is true, England seemed left out—but it was an omission that English historians hurried to make good in the 1980s.

More recently still, attention has shifted to the 'transnational' Enlightenment, to the ways in which ideas, models of behaviour, and people themselves were able to cross borders. Most recent and ambitious of all is the prospect of 'global' Enlightenment, encompassing North and South America, India, and China, as the ideas carried by European merchants, scholars, and missionaries came into dialogue with what survived of the ancient American civilizations, with the Creole Baroque, with Muslim and Hindu religious culture, and with Confucianism.

Similar pressures have extended the social dimension of the Enlightenment. Dissatisfied with a focus only on the 'high' Enlightenment of the *philosophes*, scholars have followed the example of Robert Darnton in exploring the 'low life' of Grub Street literature and publishing in Ancien Régime France.

Others have studied the institutions of everyday sociability in which ideas were discussed by all who could afford the price of entry or membership: coffee houses, reading clubs, societies for the improvement of manners, agriculture, and manufactures. Most important of all, scholars have questioned whether women's role in the Enlightenment was restricted to that of passive hostesses of salons held for the benefit of male *philosophes*. Increasingly, the focus of such studies is less on ideas for their own sake: what matters is whom they reached (and whom they excluded), and how far those who did absorb new ideas became active participants in wider processes of cultural, social and political change.

Inflationary pressure has also marked the intellectual history of Enlightenment. Observing the range of subjects of interest to the *philosophes*, or covered in the *Encyclopédie*, historians are less and less inclined to exclude any area of intellectual activity from the range of Enlightenment. Historians of science in particular have pressed the claims of their subject for inclusion. The evident presence of traditions of thought from the previous century reinforces the conclusion that it is hard to distinguish any particular set of ideas as unique to the Enlightenment. With John Pocock, many historians would rather think in terms borrowed from Wittgenstein's theory of languages, and speak of a 'family' of Enlightenment discourses, each overlapping another, but with no single element common to all.

Precisely because the Enlightenment is a historian's construction, it has been allowed to expand to fit the changing interests of modern scholarship. It is almost as if we think that something as progressive as the Enlightenment claimed to be, *ought* to have expressed every new or interesting idea, and to have embraced every good cause, which may be found in the 18th century. Not surprisingly, in the face of such variety, many scholars have concluded that it has become impossible to think of one Enlightenment, 'the' Enlightenment, and prefer instead to think of 'Enlightenments' in the plural. The construction of the Enlightenment, in other words, has ended in its deconstruction, as the pressures on its coherence become too hard to resist.

This book, however, is not written on the basis of such a counsel of scholarly despair. We do need to admit that too much has been expected of the Enlightenment, and accept that it did not embrace every new idea or advance every good cause of its time. But it can and will here be reconstructed on a more limited basis, as a distinct intellectual movement of the 18th century, dedicated to the better understanding, and thence the practical advancement, of the human condition on this earth.

In what follows, I shall work with and seek to vindicate this initial definition of the Enlightenment. (Although some scholars make an issue of the definite article before Enlightenment, I shall continue to use it when referring to the Enlightenment as a movement. Where the reference is rather to Enlightenment as a process, I shall omit the article.) The argument is made in three main chapters. Chapters 2 and 3 will be devoted to the intellectual content of the Enlightenment: one to the engagement with religion, by no means as exclusively critical as is sometimes supposed, the other to the efforts of Enlightenment thinkers to understand the conditions of human betterment, through the study of morals, history, society, and political economy. Chapter 4 will examine the social contexts of the Enlightenment, the support it received from publishers, and the ways in which Enlightenment authors sought to reach the 'public' and shape 'public opinion'; in the last, it will be argued, lay a novel approach to politics—an approach, however, which was to be swept aside rather than fulfilled by the Revolution of 1789.

The Enlightenment presented in these chapters was a European phenomenon, reaching across the entire Continent of Europe, from Britain to Transylvania, and from the Baltic to the Mediterranean. It was also an Enlightenment which extended across the Atlantic Ocean, to the European colonies in North and South America, and from the Atlantic into the Indian and Pacific Oceans, there to encounter the cultures of India and China. But the Enlightenment as I understand it remains a phenomenon of the European world. If it is possible, by analogy or translation, to construct indigenous Enlightenments in China or South Asia, or to transfer the phenomenon to quite different periods of European or world history, others may undertake the task. I will not be making the attempt here. For better or for worse, the Enlightenment was Europe's creation and legacy.

What will be attempted in Chapter 5, however, is an assessment of that legacy, by returning to the different ways in which the Enlightenment has been portrayed by philosophers and historians. Of late historians have been particularly determined to assert the Enlightenment's 'modernity', and to affirm that it 'still matters'; but it is no less important to understand why so many philosophers have differed, and have made Enlightenment the subject of critique rather than celebration.

Chapter 2
Engaging with religion

It is widely believed that the Enlightenment was hostile to religion. Sometimes Enlightenment thinkers are taken to have been against religion in general, condemning it as an irrational delusion. More common are the beliefs that the Enlightenment was particularly hostile to superstition, and hence to Roman Catholicism, that it was committed to toleration, and that it denounced the power and wealth of the clergy. Whether it is understood to have been general or specific, however, Enlightenment hostility to religion is widely regarded as a landmark in the history of 'secularization', the process whereby religious observance became an optional rather than a necessary dimension of social life.

For some time, however, scholars have been pointing out that the picture is more complicated that these clichés would allow. At the very least, the Enlightenment can be associated with a spectrum of attitudes towards religion. Those who still wish to identify Enlightenment with a fundamental critique of the rationality and coherence of religious belief now associate this with a specific 'radical Enlightenment'; the most vigorous proponent of this case, Jonathan Israel, would attach radical Enlightenment exclusively to an atheist, Spinozist metaphysics.

Other scholars, by contrast, maintain that Enlightenment had its own 'religious origins', deriving from the more intellectual strands of Protestant heterodoxy, or from reforming currents in Catholicism. From these origins, they argue, were derived Enlightenment interests in the history and social role of religion, and its commitment to tolerance of doctrinal difference. Since many who can be associated with Enlightenment manifestly retained their faith, it is not an oxymoron, such scholars assert, to think in terms of a 'religious Enlightenment'.

The problem of determining an Enlightenment attitude to religion is compounded by the extent to which its characteristic concerns were current well before the 18th century. Critical enquiry into the history of religion, along with arguments for toleration and for the subordination of church to state, were all to be found in the 17th century. One way to acknowledge this continuity has been to think in terms of an 'early Enlightenment', bridging the late 17th and early 18th centuries. In what follows, I shall adopt but qualify this suggestion. It is true that interest in those concerns intensified around 1700; but it is harder to draw a line between 'radical' and 'religious' strands of Enlightenment than has been supposed. The Enlightenment's engagement with religion represented a consolidation of the existing lines of enquiry and argument, especially those which adopted a historical approach to religion; but these were now set within a refusal to sacrifice the possibilities of life here on earth to whatever prospects might be held out on behalf of the world to come.

The Enlightenment's engagement with religion will be divided into three strands, which will be treated consecutively. The first was the historical enquiry into the nature of religion, understood as a phenomenon with a universal, 'natural' history as well as revealed or sacred histories peculiar to Jews and Christians. The second was the development of arguments for toleration. And connecting these two was a third strand: reflection on the relation between the sacred and the civil, this too increasingly approached through history.

Enquiry into natural and revealed religion in the 17th century

Key to understanding the continuities between the 17th century and Enlightenment enquiries into the history and role of religion is the distinction between the spheres of nature and revelation. All Christians agreed that theirs was a revealed religion, and that by revelation, as recorded in the Bible—the Word of God—mankind could know that Christ's sacrifice had secured the possibility of their salvation, by the operation of divine grace. But Christians were also agreed that God had ordained that mankind live within the natural order which he had created. The natural order had its own code of behaviour, known as the 'law of nature', which applied to all humans, whether or not they acknowledged the revelation of which Moses had been the intermediary for the Hebrews, and which Christ had declared to all mankind. Obedience to the natural law would not bring salvation; but it was nonetheless a duty which all mankind owed to God by virtue of their creation.

A corollary of separating nature from revelation was that not only law but religion itself could be understood as universal, 'natural' to man. Just as all men could be supposed to be subject to the law of nature, so all men naturally professed religion and worshipped God, whether or not they were beneficiaries of a specific revelation. In these terms, 'natural religion' was both a proposition about God's relation to the world, and a description of human religious practices.

In the former guise, natural religion was assumed to be compatible with revelation: both affirmed that the world and all living things were a divine 'creation': matter had not always existed, as some ancient Greek philosophers had suggested. Moreover, far from being undermined by the scientific discoveries of the 17th century, the proposition of a creator God had been reinforced: the more extensive and detailed man's understanding of nature, the more nature gave evidence of God's original design. Newton's pronouncement to this effect was only the most authoritative of many. Even those who dissented, and continued to entertain the eternity of matter, such as Spinoza, did so in a form which identified Nature with God: in Spinoza's terms, God and Nature were but two 'modes' of one 'substance'. Spinoza's materialism, although abhorrent to the great majority of Christian natural philosophers, did not prevent him being a proponent of a natural theology.

In its second guise, as a description of religious practices, natural religion was most safely explained in the same way as natural law, as an expression of human reason. But it might equally be explained as an expression of the human passions. As in the case of natural law, ancient philosophy and poetry provided a rich repertoire of examples of natural religious belief. Many illustrated the Epicurean conviction, elaborated by the Roman poet Lucretius, that religion was a product of fear of unknown forces. Another ancient manifestation of natural religious belief was the tendency to worship great men and women, deifying them after, or even before, their natural deaths: the phenomenon known as 'euhemerism'.

Of course, under the first and second of the Ten Commandments, all alien religious practices were 'idolatry', and Christians had long condemned them as the work of the devil. But to explain idolatry as a manifestation of natural religion (rather than as demonic) was by no means necessarily to compromise revelation. The idea that the growing interest in natural religion indicated a weakening conviction of the superior truth of Christianity is very wide of the mark. On the contrary, an understanding of pagan beliefs and practices as 'natural' made it much easier for Christian missionaries to the non-European world to devise coherent strategies of conversion. Among scholars, meanwhile, the idea that all men were naturally religious facilitated a growing interest in the comparative study of religions, a form of enquiry closed to

Christians as long as all religions other than Christianity (and possibly Judaism and Islam) were regarded as instruments of the devil.

If it was possible for both Catholics and Protestants to expand the scope of moral and religious enquiry under the rubric of nature, the matter of revelation was, unsurprisingly, much more divisive. But here too there was, by the end of the 17th century, a turn to history. By then it was clear that Protestants and Catholics were as divided among themselves as between each other over the understanding of grace and of man's potential contribution to salvation. As they turned to the early Church, and to the Fathers in particular, to clarify their differences, scholars discovered that a historical approach might also put those differences in perspective. A sense of perspective was further encouraged by histories of ancient philosophy, Near Eastern as well as Greek and Roman, which led to the realization that several of the more complex Christian doctrines, such as the immortality of the soul, or the Trinity, had borrowed their metaphysics from pagan sources. Some, notably the Socinians, drew heterodox conclusions from such scholarship, questioning the divinity of Christ; but its principal effect was to demonstrate that doctrinal differences had been a recurrent feature of Christianity, and were best approached through its history.

Historical reassessment of revelation became necessary for another, no less important reason. For not only had the understanding of grace and related doctrines fragmented, the documentary evidence of revelation, the Bible itself, was also loosed from its moorings. Since the Reformation, both sides had insisted on the integrity of Scripture. Reformers claimed that their translations of the Bible had given believers direct access to the Word of God; in response, the Council of Trent had vested the authority of the Roman Catholic Church in the Vulgate Bible, Jerome's Latin translation from the Hebrew 'Old Testament' and Greek New Testament. By the second half of the 17th century, however,

Biblical scholars were raising more and more questions over the stability and interpretation of the text. The process reached a climax in the two decades before 1700, with the publication of major works of Biblical criticism by two French scholars, the Catholic Richard Simon (1638–1712), and the Protestant Jean Le Clerc (1657–1736), a Huguenot émigré in Holland.

The issues were several. As Simon observed in his magisterial *Histoire critique du Vieux Testament* (1678, 1684), there was no original text of the Bible. There was therefore no benchmark against which to test the reliability of the earliest known versions, Hebrew and Greek, and every likelihood that textual corruption had occurred. Authorship of the Bible was a second problem, since it could not be assumed from the names of the books. In particular it was most unlikely that Moses could have written the entire Pentateuch. Still more complication attached to the languages of the Bible. Not only were there Greek and Hebrew versions of the Old Testament, the late addition of vowel points to the Hebrew version may have altered its meaning. Le Clerc's studies in particular suggested that Hebrew usage had changed over time, indicating that the text was a composite of sources from different periods. A final difficulty concerned the Bible's chronologies. Not only did different versions offer differing calculations of the age of the world—estimates varying from just under 4,000 to almost 7,000 years between Creation and the birth of Christ. But the chronologies within the Bible proved impossible to reconcile.

The implications of these findings were potentially far-reaching. As a composite text, existing in several versions, the Bible was not the univocal Word of God. Revelation did not have a consistent documentary basis. A range of conclusions might be drawn. Simon aspired to produce a new, critical edition of the text which the Catholic Church could declare to be authoritative. But this was at best naïve: in the 1680s the Roman Catholic authorities decided to reject the findings of Biblical scholarship, and Simon's works were placed on the Index of Prohibited Books. Le Clerc, following Hugo Grotius (1583–1645), took the Bible to be a historical text of a historically specific religion: it was the duty of Christians to continue to discuss its meaning, not accept it as a dogmatic *fait accompli*. But he too met opposition from orthodox, literally minded Calvinists.

The historical particularity of the Bible was reinforced by new scholarship on other peoples of the ancient Near East, the Egyptians and the Chaldeans or Assyrians, neighbours and at times masters of the Hebrews. These had different chronologies, which suggested a world older than the Mosaic creation story would allow. But their chronologies, along with those to be found in ancient Greek writings, could also help to make sense of those in the Bible: it was clear that a coherent historical narrative would need to combine sacred and pagan evidence. The authors of such findings, prominent among them the English scholars John Marsham, John Spencer, Thomas Hyde, and Thomas Stanley, did not regard them as undermining the Bible. But they not only provided matter for the comparative study of religion; they strengthened the tendency to understand the Bible, and hence revelation, in historical perspective.

Early Enlightenment

Interest in these lines of enquiry intensified around 1700, and in several cases acquired a new critical edge. The 'early Enlightenment' critics of religion, however, differed widely in their arguments, and were often indebted for them to earlier scholarship which had no radical motivation.

Among the first to see the potential of the findings of Biblical scholarship was Spinoza, in his *Tractatus theologico-politicus* (*Theological-Political Treatise*) (1670). Spinoza was clear that the Bible (by which he meant chiefly the Hebrew Bible) had not been written by Moses and those who gave their names to its books; it had been compiled by the high-priest Ezra after the Babylonian exile. As such, it should be read as the historical narrative of a particular people, the ancient Hebrews, and of the laws by which they had organized themselves. By taking their narrative to be the Word of God, however, the Hebrews had made it a manual of instruction in piety and obedience: in other words, in justice and love of one's neighbour, the prerequisites of sociable living. The Bible could not offer a true knowledge of God, which was attainable only through a philosophical understanding of Nature. The Bible's significance, rather, was precisely as sacred *history*. For Jews and Christians, the Bible was the historical key to understanding the moral and political foundations of society in *this* world, not the next.

A different use of new approaches to the understanding of religion was made by Pierre Bayle (1647–1706) who, like Jean Le Clerc, was a Huguenot exile in the United Provinces. In his first major work, *Pensées diverses sur le Comète* (*Divers Thoughts on the Comet*) (1682), Bayle took up the issue of idolatry. The widespread view that comets were portents, evident once again in the popular response to the comet of 1680, suggested that idolatry was still rampant. Observing that idolatry could not be pleasing to the true God, Bayle wondered whether atheism was really any worse. After all, few if any conducted their life according to their professed principles; fallen man lived by his passions. Selfish as those passions were, they could only be satisfied in society. Atheists, therefore, were at least as sociable as idolaters. The only difference between them would be that atheists would not worship false gods, but would live openly by their passions.

Bayle was the master of the argument that cut several ways at once. Ostensibly, the 'atheist' hypothesis had no bearing at all on true Christians. But Christians of different confessions routinely condemned others as 'idolaters' (a point Bayle underlined by writing anonymously in the guise of a Catholic), while, as we have seen, all non-Christian peoples awaiting conversion were by nature idolaters. With some justification, therefore, Bayle's equation of atheists and idolaters was taken to question the foundations of natural as well as revealed religion, and thus the necessity of religion to human society—a step that even Spinoza had not taken.

A radical of a different stripe was John Toland (1670–1722), the Irish intellectual adventurer, republican, friend of the Electress Sophia of Hanover (mother of King George I of England), ghostwriter, and freethinker. Toland made a virtue of eclecticism in all things political and intellectual, but above all in his irreligion. As suited the occasion, he combined materialist metaphysics with selective appropriation of modern Biblical, Patristic, and natural religious scholarship. He began with *Christianity not Mysterious* (1695–6), a work taken to be anti-Trinitarian, but whose central claim was simply that the 'mystery' of Christianity was a clerical fraud: Scripture was open to be read by anyone possessed of reason.

A succession of works over the following two decades illustrated this proposition in relation to Old and New Testaments. *Origines Judaicae* (1709) argued that Moses had used religion as an instrument of policy, and that his understanding of it was originally Egyptian rather than Hebrew; it had not included the doctrine of the immortal soul. Turning to the New Testament, in works such as *Amyntor* (1699) and *Nazarenus* (1718), Toland advertised the uncertainties over the canon of its books, and made a mischievous case for the genuineness of the supposed 'Gospel of Barnabas' (parts of which supported the Islamic view of Christ). All of these provoked furious responses from orthodox and heterodox theologians alike, responses which added notoriety to Toland's arguments. Toland was equally adept in his subversion of natural religion: *A Specimen of a Critical History of the Druids* (1726) compared the Druids favourably with Christian clergy, while still treating Druid practices as priestcraft and superstition.

Toland's efforts were afforced within the British Isles by a group of freethinkers, including Anthony Collins, Matthew Tindal, and John Trenchard. Collins put his extensive library at the disposal of Toland and others, and in his own *Discourse of Freethinking* (1713) argued on materialist, necessitarian grounds against free will and the immortal soul. Trenchard's *Natural History of Superstition* (1709) turned the idea that religion had a natural as well as a revealed history into a straightforward attack on priestcraft, while Tindal's *Christianity as old as Creation* (1730) collapsed grace into nature by arguing that Christ's message was no more than a reiteration of the pure law of nature which had obtained before the Fall. Collectively Toland and his associates were once characterized as 'Deists', believers in a God but not in Christ; more recently this label has fallen out of use among historians, a reflection of the greater awareness that natural and revealed religion were complementary, and that the radicals drew on the scholarship devoted to both.

Other, interconnecting circles of the irreligious were active on the Continent of Europe over the first four decades of the 18th century. At the heart of these was the shadowy group responsible for the most famous of all critiques of established religions, the *Treatise of the Three Impostors*, a composite of several works assembled and first published in French as *La vie et l'esprit de Spinosa* (1719) before being reissued as the *Traité des trois imposteurs* in 1721. The initial title accurately identified the book as containing a biography of Spinoza, along with a translation of a section of Spinoza's posthumously published *Ethics* (1677). To these were added selections from several other irreligious texts, drawn from an older, more direct tradition of irreligion: it was in this vein that Moses, Christ, and Mahomet were identified as impostors who had deceived their peoples. This eclectic textual mix was the creation of Jean Rousset de Missy, Jean Aymon, and Charles Levier, all Huguenots in exile in Holland, and members of a secret society called the Knights of Jubilation; Toland and Collins were among their British connections. Although interested in the philosophy of Spinoza, the editors of the *Three Impostors* simplified its materialism; if this was the Enlightenment at its most radical, it was not strictly Spinozist.

From the United Provinces radiated circuits of freethinkers and sympathetic publishers, ready to pass on copies of fugitive publications such as the *Three Impostors*, as well as manuscript copies and translations of other irreligious writings which were too dangerous to publish. Their most important destination was France, where the Comte de Boulainvilliers was, until his death in 1722, a particularly active sympathizer and disseminator of such literature. Other circles of radical freethinking existed in Germany, and to a much lesser extent in Italy.

Assessment of their significance is not as straightforward as some sympathetic historians have supposed. Precisely because the publications were fugitive and the circulation clandestine, the reach of these works was limited. They were also on different levels of intellectual sophistication, and hence their potential contribution to original argument about religion was uneven. Copies of several of these works were owned by or accessible to Voltaire, Diderot, and D'Holbach, but the arguments of these *philosophes* would by no means simply echo those found in the earlier clandestine literature.

For it is misleading to focus exclusively on the 'radical', irreligious Enlightenment as the outcome of the extended enquiry into natural and revealed religion pursued by scholars and theologians from 1650 onwards. Equally an outcome of that enquiry were the seven volumes of the *Religious Ceremonies of the World* (1723–37), by the engraver Bernard Picart and the publisher Jean Frederic Bernard (Figure 3). The collaborators were French Protestant exiles in the United Provinces who saw an opportunity to popularize the findings of the accumulating scholarship on natural and revealed religion. In successive, overlapping volumes they covered Judaism, Roman Catholicism, the religions of the Americas, India, Asia

3. The principal religions of the world. Frontispiece to *Cérémonies et coutumes religieuses de tous les peuples du monde*, by Bernard Picart and Jean Frederic Bernard (1723). Not a work of scholarship as such, this compilation exemplified a new curiosity about the religions of the world, and gave its readers access to information about them which had been gathered by travellers and missionaries.

(China and Japan), and Africa, Greek Orthodoxy, Protestants, including Anglicans and heterodox groups, and finally Islam. The book was a commercial success, and was translated into Dutch, German, and English. But it was not hostile to religion, as even historians partial to radical Enlightenment have been obliged to admit.

Intellectually much more impressive were the contrasting uses of the new scholarship made by two Neapolitans, the historian Pietro Giannone (1676–1748) and the philosopher Giambattista Vico (1668–1744) (Figure 4). Giannone's *Triregno* (*The Three Kingdoms*) was written while its author was in exile in Vienna between 1731 and 1733. The three kingdoms were respectively the earthly kingdom of the Old Testament Hebrews, the heavenly kingdom offered by Christ's mission, and the Papal kingdom to which that offer had been reduced by the Church, which had betrayed Christ's other-worldly purpose. The seizure of the manuscript by agents of the Holy Office, following Giannone's kidnap and imprisonment in Savoy, ensured the work's subversive

4. **Giambattista Vico (1668–1744), Neapolitan philosopher. His *New Science* (1725, 1744) was one of the most enigmatic works of the century, but by 1800 it was recognized as an extraordinarily imaginative contribution to the philosophy of history.**

reputation among historians. But the work could not have been written without the development of scholarly understanding of the Bible, the ancient Near East, and the early Church since the middle of the previous century.

By contrast, Vico was able to publish his *Scienza nuova* (*New Science of the Nature of Nations*). The first edition appeared in 1725, and new, revised editions followed in 1730 and 1744, the last becoming the one by which the work is generally known. The novelty of Vico's 'science' was that it applied specifically to man, independent of nature. It was a philosophy of history, which proposed that the development of the peoples or 'nations' of the earth had occurred through the regular operation of divine providence, and followed a recognizable pattern. But it was the earliest phases of this development which most interested Vico. The key to the mind of the earliest men, he argued, lay not in supposing that they followed a universal natural law, but in studying their poetry and religious mythology. Men had used their imaginations before their reason. Famously, Vico argued that the poetry of Homer was not the work of a single author, but a rendering of the collective memory of the ancient Greek people. This was an insight he shared with and perhaps derived from French scholars, but he alone set it within a larger argument for the historical significance of poetry and myth for an understanding of the historical development of society.

Vico called his new science a 'rational civil theology of divine providence', and framed it in opposition to specific predecessors. Against the Grotian hypothesis that natural law would obtain even without the existence of God, Vico insisted that it was divine providence which had enabled men to appreciate the existence of a 'common sense' of moral value, underlying the separate laws of individual nations. At the same time, Vico's conception of divine providence as an expression of God's 'ordinary power' (a Scholastic category) repudiated the Spinozist idea of a monist, all-determining 'nature'. Most sharply of all, Vico rejected Bayle's hypothesis of a society of atheists, arguing that in the absence of revelation (confined to the ancient Hebrews), the formation of society was inconceivable without idolatry—the worship of a God out of fear of the forces of nature.

By characterizing his as a 'civil' theology, Vico sought autonomy for the social from the realms of nature and grace alike; but it was still a 'theology', the operation of divine providence being a truth, not a hypothesis. Given his denunciations of 'modern', especially Cartesian and Epicurean philosophy, Vico is difficult to class as an adherent of Enlightenment. Yet so complex and fertile an engagement with Grotius, Spinoza, and Bayle was not the work of a thinker at odds with his time. Even as he proclaimed his Catholic orthodoxy, Vico was taking historical enquiry into the origin and uses of religion in new and remarkably original directions.

'The Enlightenment Bible'

By 1740, in any case, it seems that the critical scholarship which fed the early Enlightenment was losing its edge. On key issues, such as Biblical chronology and Mosaic authorship of the Pentateuch, criticism had failed to come up with convincing alternatives. Both Vico and Giannone continued to interpret history within the Vulgate chronology which allowed just 4,000 years between the Creation and the birth of Christ. Giannone even accepted the Mosaic authorship of the Pentateuch, on the basis offered by Simon. If anything, developments in scholarship in the 18th century tended to reinforce the Bible's status as the revealed Word of God. In his *Conjectures on Genesis* (1753), Jean Astruc confirmed the hypothesis that the book derived from a number of different sources, but did not deny that Moses had composed it.

In Germany, Biblical scholarship had an accepted place within the Lutheran universities. The greatest Biblical scholar of the century, Johann David Michaelis (1717–91), accumulated an unprecedented quantity of linguistic and ethnographic evidence to inform understanding of the text. Some of this derived from an ambitious scholarly expedition to Egypt and Arabia between 1761 and 1767, which the Danish court had sponsored, and whose research questions Michaelis had framed. (But in which he wisely did not take part; only one of the original five scholars returned alive.) For Michaelis such evidence confirmed the historical truth of the Bible, even if its text had been corrupted.

A historical perspective also informed the interpretation of the Bible by the leading German Jewish scholar and philosopher, Moses Mendelssohn, who produced a new German translation (in Hebrew letters) of the Pentateuch, *The Book of the Paths of Peace* (1779–83). Denying that the addition of the vowel points to the Hebrew text had been an inlet to corruption, Mendelssohn held them up as having preserved the original meaning of the oral text. The significance of the Pentateuch was precisely that it recorded historical fact, the establishment of Judaism as a national religion based on pure natural religion, with none of the extravagances added by Christian revelation.

By the end of the 18th century, therefore, a historical understanding of the Bible had taken a firm hold. The critical Bible of the 17th century had become what a recent historian has termed 'the Enlightenment Bible'. With rare exceptions, however, the Enlightenment Bible was no more likely than its predecessor to undermine revelation.

Enlightenment histories of religion

Alongside the Enlightenment Bible, interest in the comparative study of religion was even more characteristic of the later Enlightenment. Here the scope for subversive implication was greater, but was by no means at the forefront of every enquiry.

Voltaire (1694–1778) led the way in the *Essai sur les moeurs et l'esprit des nations* (1756). The scope of the work is better captured in the title of the English translation, *Essay on Universal History* (1782); it was framed as a response to the *Universal History* (1681) of Bishop Bossuet. Voltaire's first move was to repudiate the traditional Jewish and Christian starting point of world history. Instead, he began his history in China, whose chronologies indicated a nation considerably older than the Biblical Hebrews. Thence he worked his way back westwards, devoting chapters to India and Islamic Arabia before he came to Israel and Christian Europe. In each case there were accompanying chapters on the major religions: Confucianism (treated effectively as a religion), Hinduism, Islam, Judaism, and Christianity. That the last two followed Islam, historically their offspring, only underlined Voltaire's determination to disrupt the order of Jewish and Christian sacred history.

Voltaire's understanding of Confucianism and Hinduism as religions was, even so, heavily dependent on the findings of Jesuit missionaries to China and India, findings informed by their conception of natural religion, and their assumption that the Eastern religions were monotheist. But Voltaire departed from his Jesuit sources in treating those religions as culturally differentiated. No longer were they manifestations of a common, natural idolatry, more or less distant from conversion to Christianity; the great monotheisms of the world were products of individual historical circumstances.

Rather more subversive in implication was David Hume, whose *Natural History of Religion* (1757) abstracted from historical narrative altogether. Hume challenged not simply Jewish and Christian sacred history, but the priority of monotheism. According to 'the natural progress of human thought', Hume conjectured, polytheism or idolatry must have been the original religion of men. To which he added that 'the theism, and that too not entirely pure, of one or two nations, form no objection worth regarding', a dismissal of the Biblical Hebrews which did not even bother to name them.

Originally, indeed, polytheists were 'really a kind of superstitious atheists'; the distinction between idolaters and atheists was redundant. It was only as nations had elevated one god above others as their tutelary deity that they had become monotheists. Considered as religious types, polytheism encouraged superstition, while monotheism tended to 'enthusiasm' or fanaticism. In their enthusiasm, monotheists were characteristically less tolerant than polytheists, and adopted systems of morality opposed to those men naturally possess. Hume strongly implied that no monotheism was worse in these respects than Christianity, whose votaries supported their elevation of the next world above the present with a morality of self-denial, the antithesis of what we naturally find 'useful and agreeable' in this world.

Although Hume was probably unaware of it at the time he wrote this essay, the idea of 'natural history' was itself transformed by the publication in 1749 of the first three volumes of the *Histoire naturelle, générale et particulière* by the Comte de Buffon (1707–88). Buffon's great work had contrasting implications for Jewish and Christian sacred history and the history of religions more generally. In the case of sacred history, it was apparent that Buffon's understanding of the natural history of the world required a much longer time-span than that allowed by any Biblical calculation of the time elapsed since Creation. Although Buffon initially denied any intention to contradict Scripture, he would concede in 1778 that creation must have occurred between 75,000 and three million years ago. He suggested that since Nature's chronology did not admit of the same precision as civil chronology, the two might be detached, making it possible to continue to use the Bible's chronology to frame human history, from remote antiquity to the present. Nevertheless, the unity of sacred history as an account of the beginning of the world and its first people had been sundered.

For the history of religions, by contrast, Buffon's *Natural History* offered a new point of departure, by underlining the extent and importance of natural catastrophe in the making of the world. There had been no single, universal Flood; but disasters must repeatedly have required the earliest humans to regroup. One of the first to develop the insight was Nicolas-Antoine Boulanger (1722–59), in *L'Antiquité dévoilée—Antiquity unveiled by its Practices, or a Critical Examination of the Principal Religious and Political Opinions, Ceremonies and Institutions of the different peoples of the Earth* (1766).

Boulanger's starting point—that the Flood had eliminated any traces of earlier human existence, and was therefore when history must be taken to begin—was not in itself original: humanist historical scholars had made the point since the 16th century. But Boulanger now focused attention specifically on the variety of religious practices which men had developed in response to that emblematic catastrophe. Among these he identified commemorative, funerary, and liturgical ceremonies, mystery cults, and cyclical patterns of worship, for each of which he provided detailed descriptive accounts drawn from the full range of known world religions. It was no longer a question of whether these practices were to be thought of as idolatry. Instead, Boulanger argued that study of religious traditions offered a far better insight into the nature of man than the rational suppositions of philosophers, metaphysicians, and jurists. Here was the true introduction to 'the history of man in society'.

Boulanger's work was published after his death by his friend the Baron D'Holbach (1723–89). D'Holbach was (in private) a professed atheist, who like Spinoza combined an interest in the history of religion with a materialist philosophy, set out in his *Système de la Nature* (1770). But D'Holbach's materialism differed from Spinoza's in being founded on sense experience, the philosophy endorsed by D'Alembert in the *Discours préliminaire* to the *Encyclopédie*. His atheism was thus qualified by the limits to what could and could not be known; and the test of that was historical enquiry. For D'Holbach (as indeed for Spinoza), history supplied the framework necessary to understand religion.

This line of enquiry culminated in the extension of Boulanger's approach to ancient religious practices to take in the evidence of poetry and mythology. That these might be the key to the mental universe of the first men was of course the great insight of Vico. But the *New Science* and its author remained unknown outside Naples until late in the century, when his insight was taken up by the greatest historical philosopher of the German Enlightenment, J. G. Herder (1744–1803), and by Francesco Mario Pagano (1748–99), a leading figure in the late Neapolitan Enlightenment.

Herder did so in an extended study of the poetry of the Bible, *On the Spirit of Hebrew Poetry* (1782). The form of Biblical poetry had long been a subject of scholarly debate, a debate recently taken to a higher plane by the suggestion of the English scholar, Robert Lowth (1710–87), that it exhibited 'parallelism' rather than metre or rhyme. For Herder, however, the significance of Hebrew poetry went beyond its technical character. It was among the earliest national literatures, and as such a key to understanding the Hebrew people.

Pagano, like Boulanger, cast his net wider. Despite its unassuming title, his *Saggi politici* (*Political Essays*) (1783–5, 1791–2) offered a philosophical account of the whole course of human history, but with most attention to the earliest formation of societies, understood through their religions and mythologies. Repeatedly citing Vico as well as Buffon, Boulanger, and the Scottish historians Hume, Robertson, and Ferguson, Pagano's achievement was to be, in effect, the Enlightenment's Vico. After Vico, it was Pagano who most fully realized the potential of the history of religion for the history of society, connecting it with what I will argue in Chapter 3 was the central, defining concern of Enlightenment thought: the 'progress of society'.

Arguments for toleration in the name of civil peace

A second strand of Enlightenment engagement with religion was a contribution to the case for toleration. As a response to religious difference, the idea of toleration long preceded the Enlightenment. It had first emerged in Europe some 200 years earlier, as a pragmatic response by the civil authorities to the religious violence unleashed by the Reformation. To be sure, early modern European rulers expected to enforce religious uniformity among their subjects, and were quite prepared to go to war to enforce their own confessional allegiance on others. But when a ruler was unable to enforce uniformity, and the community divided, the consequences might endanger something even more valuable than confessional uniformity—the maintenance of civil peace.

Exemplary of the damage which such conflict might inflict were the French Wars of Religion, which began around 1560, when a sudden increase in the numbers of Protestants provoked a ferocious reaction from Catholics. A decade of killings had culminated in the dreadful Massacre of St Bartholomew in Paris in 1572, when victims were torn limb from limb and the dead bodies of Protestants mutilated as they lay on the ground.

As the conflict dragged on, both moderate Protestants and *politique* Catholics had looked to the monarchy to impose a settlement on the warring parties by granting a greater or lesser degree of 'toleration' to the Huguenot minority. Such a settlement was eventually made possible by the succession of the Protestant Henry of Navarre to the throne, and his conversion to Catholicism; he then issued the Edict of Nantes (1598) granting security to his former co-religionists. But the Edict was far from establishing a general principle of toleration, on civil or religious grounds: its rationale was accommodation of specific confessional differences, for as long as it might be necessary to preserve the civil peace. The 'Revocation' of the Edict by Louis XIV a little short of a hundred years later, in 1685, was a reminder that once a ruler was confident of his power to enforce civil peace, he might revert to the policy of confessional uniformity, and persecute the dissident minority.

The limitations of the *politique* case for toleration were explored by the greatest political philosopher of the 17th century, Thomas Hobbes (1588–1679). In both *De cive* (1642) and *Leviathan* (1651) Hobbes argued that the maintenance of any society required a single, unqualified sovereign power, with authority to determine the public expression of opinion in all matters which might disturb the peace. Religion was clearly one of these, and Hobbes took the clergy to present the greatest of all threats to peace. Hobbes reinforced his primary argument by reference to sacred history, which he interpreted as demonstrating that first the Jewish then the Christian religions had been instituted, at God's command, under the authority of the civil power. Christians in particular had no good reason, natural or revealed, to challenge the sovereign's judgement in matters of religious (or any other) opinion. Scholars now debate whether Hobbes also thought that the sovereign might use its authority to tolerate variety of forms of worship, as the Commonwealth did in England after 1649, a position apparently endorsed by a passage in *Leviathan*; but his overriding principle remained the sovereign's power to determine a common form of worship, in the interest of civil peace.

A subtler treatment of the same theme emerged from Spinoza's *Theologico-Political Treatise* of 1670. Written in direct response to persecution of his heterodox Christian friends by the Dutch Calvinists, the work was framed as a demonstration that the 'freedom to philosophize' presented no danger to piety and the stability of the state. Arguing, as we have seen, that the role of the Jewish as of the Christian religion was to promote piety and obedience, the requisites of sociability, Spinoza maintained that the Hebrews' priests had never exercised authority at the expense of the civil power. This was reinforced by his metaphysics: since

God is identified with Nature, the freer and fuller the investigation of Nature, the closer the individual would come to God. The idea that there should be a *libertas philosophandi* was not itself new, and was not the same as religious toleration, but in Spinoza's hands it became an argument for the fullest possible liberty to think, to pursue understanding and to know God, compatible with the peace of society.

The arguments of Hobbes and Spinoza were the culmination of a phase of debate dominated by the memory of religious war, when most Christians still believed that their particular church preached the one true doctrine. Toleration, in this perspective, was no more than a recognition that civil peace might depend on sanctioning the simultaneous expression of opposing religious beliefs, while keeping them sufficiently apart to prevent open conflict.

Protestant arguments for toleration

By the late 17th century, there was a new context for the debate, created by the Revocation of the Edict of Nantes in 1685. Driven into exile in the United Provinces, the intellectual leadership of the Huguenot *réfuge* sought to rally the powers of Europe to resist the French King. For the most part, however, they did so in terms which deliberately avoided any call to renew religious war, but instead offered arguments for religious toleration.

Two texts in particular made the case. One was the *Letter on Toleration* by John Locke (1632–1704), written after 1685 and published in Latin and in English in 1689. Locke had first discussed toleration in an essay in the 1660s, when he had reached a Hobbesian conclusion in favour of the sovereign's power to enforce uniformity in the name of peace. Forced into exile in the United Provinces in the early 1680s because of his association with opponents of Charles II, Locke found himself in a new and much more complex predicament. In England, James II was embarking on a policy of toleration, but one whose object was the toleration of Roman Catholics alongside Protestant Dissenters, the better to undermine the Church of England. In the United Provinces, Locke had close friends among the Huguenot exiles, who in turn were associated with the Dutch Remonstrants (the heirs of Grotius), who were under continuous pressure from the stricter Calvinists.

Faced with such complexity, Locke continued to insist on the requirement of civil order: under the law of nature all men have an obligation to preserve themselves and others, and this requires the institution, by agreement, of a civil authority with jurisdiction to preserve peace in this world. But the law of nature also obliges all men to worship God in religious communities of their choosing, over which the civil authority has no legitimate jurisdiction. Individual Christians therefore had the duty, and the right, to worship in the manner they believed would conduce to their salvation.

This was an argument for pluralism, against any established church; but it was also an exclusive, Protestant argument. Locke notoriously added the riders that neither Roman Catholics nor atheists should be tolerated, Catholics because they were subjects of a foreign as well as their native sovereign, atheists because their promises would be without higher guarantee. The deeper Protestantism of his argument, however, was its assumption that the individual Christian was responsible for him or herself before God. In the Roman Catholic perspective, this was (and still is) to impose an intolerable burden on the individual: it was for the Church to intercede on his or her behalf before God. For all its lasting fame, Locke's *Letter on Toleration* did not set the argument for toleration on a universal basis: its foundation was divinely inspired natural law, interpreted on Protestant terms.

Pierre Bayle had been driven into exile under even greater threat to his own life than Locke, for he had converted to Catholicism, then recanted; and his brother had died for his Protestant faith. Nevertheless, Bayle refused to support the call for resistance made by the leader of the Huguenots in exile, Pierre Jurieu. Arguing instead that tolerance was the only Christian response to religious difference, Bayle insisted that a strong state was its prerequisite. But on no account should the state use its strength to enforce religious uniformity.

In the *Commentaire philosophique* (1686–8) Bayle framed this argument as an extended series of reflections on Christ's injunction to 'compel them to come in' (Luke 14:23). The use of force in an effort to convert those who disagree simply encourages the use of force in reply; and of all religions, the doctrines of Christianity are the least compatible with violence, the most damaged by its exercise. Against fellow Protestants as much as Roman Catholics, Bayle insisted that Christianity depended on liberty of the individual conscience. The 'natural light' of reason or conscience in every individual was the standard of judgement; any strongly held belief should be respected.

Underlying Bayle's arguments for tolerance and liberty of conscience was his deeper scepticism about the extent to which opinion determined the behaviour of human beings. Given that their passions, not their beliefs, made men and women sociable, any attempt to enforce a particular set of religious opinions upon them would distort the operation of their passions, with disastrous results for social peace. Bayle's scepticism also suggested that no opinion was necessarily better than any other; apart from the Christian revelation (for those who accepted it), there was no universal criterion of truth, in philosophy or religion. This was not Locke's argument, but it too followed the logic of Protestantism, placing the burden of faith on the individual, and arguing that the individual must decide what his or her faith entailed, as long as the peace of society was not endangered.

Toleration from Voltaire to the Declaration of the Rights of Man

It was arguably in transcending the confessional divide that a distinct Enlightenment contribution to the case for toleration was elaborated. A crucial, very public intervention was made by Voltaire, in his *Traité sur la tolérance* (1763). Its context was the notorious trial of the Huguenot merchant, Jean Calas, condemned to death by the Parlement of Toulouse in 1762 for the alleged murder of his son (Figure 5). The trial reflected the continued precariousness of the Huguenots' position within France; even if *de facto* tolerance was widespread, they remained vulnerable to panics and popular pressure on the authorities, typified by this case. Voltaire's response, however, was not based on particular sympathy for those he had recently described as

5. **Jean Calas on the scaffold (1762). The engraving depicts Calas being comforted before his limbs were broken on the wheel, after which he was executed by strangulation. Voltaire made the treatment of Calas emblematic of the horrors of religious intolerance.**

'wretched Huguenots'. He put his argument in terms which had no theological premises.

The *Treatise* was deliberately unsystematic, its tone mocking. Since the Reformation, Voltaire remarked, it was religious fanatics who had been the greatest disturbers of the peace of society in France. Persecuted by the Catholics, the Huguenots had resisted with violence. It was possible that tolerance would provoke them no less than persecution—but hardly likely. Moreover, circumstances had changed: governments were stronger, while society was gentler. Manners had softened, and philosophy had disarmed superstition. The present was an age of reason, and reason was 'the one slow but infallible route towards enlightenment'. In short, intolerance of the kind so cruelly displayed by the judges in the Calas case was simply anachronistic, a throwback to an earlier age.

Voltaire supported his argument with selective historical examples, showing that the ancients—Greeks, Romans, Hebrews, and even Christ himself—had been more tolerant than the Christians had ever been. But his primary point was that tolerance was a matter of manners, not of individual conscience: civilization was characterized by, and depended upon, tolerance of religious difference. His argument was historical, not theological or even strictly philosophical. As societies became more civilized, their members learned to treat each other with greater respect, informed by an understanding of the behaviour of the ancient Greeks and Romans, and indeed of Christ's own teaching. This process of enlightenment should be allowed to continue, not defied by backward-looking judges whose religious prejudices threatened the peace of society.

Such confidence in the historical process of enlightenment has been betrayed too often since to stand as a sufficient argument for toleration; beside the writings of Locke or Bayle, Voltaire's *Treatise* may appear shallow. But theirs, as we have seen, were Protestant arguments for toleration, unlikely to be acceptable on theological grounds to Catholics, let alone non-Christians. By contrast, Voltaire's realization that theology must be set aside, and nothing more be considered than 'the physical and moral well-being of society', coupled with his confidence that a well-mannered society mocked fanaticism, resulted in an exclusively this-worldly argument for toleration.

Further arguments emerged in the last quarter of the 18th century. By then, many of Europe's most powerful rulers, among them the King of Prussia and the Emperor and head of the Austrian monarchy, had been persuaded to implement measures of toleration on economic grounds; while interests of state were still paramount, there was no longer a conviction that enforcement of religious uniformity was essential to social order. In Berlin, Moses Mendelssohn took advantage of the King's liberalism to argue in *Jerusalem* (1783) that tolerance be extended to Jewish worship and ceremonies on the ground of individual liberty of conscience, adding later that the Jews should be recognized as forming a voluntary society without coercive powers, hence as no threat to the state. Belatedly, even the French monarchy admitted its mistake in revoking the Edict of Nantes, issuing an Edict of Toleration in 1787, granting Protestants civil rights, though still not the right of public worship.

More positive inspiration was offered by the rebellion in the British American colonies, which repudiated the established Church of England in the name of religious freedom independent of the civil power, and deployed a language of universal rights to justify the colonists' stance. Their example prompted Dissenters in England to recognize the limitations of Locke's earlier advocacy of toleration, and to extend to Roman Catholics the natural right to worship in the religious community of one's choice. Although this reflected a diminishing fear (in mainland Britain) that Catholics were a threat to the state, it helped to generalize, or at least to deconfessionalize, the idea of toleration.

The Declaration of the Rights of Man and Citizens issued in August 1789 at the start of the French Revolution had the same implication: the National Assembly almost immediately recognized that this entailed a general freedom to worship, and followed up with political rights for Protestants by the end of the year, and for Jews in another two years. The argument from the rights of man was built on few visible foundations: in the words of the American Declaration of Independence, its truths were 'self-evident'. But once accepted, the idea that there are rights which are equal and universal for all men (and women) led very quickly to toleration and religious freedom. It is one of the thinnest but also one of the most appealing arguments for religious toleration, and its enunciation may be traced to the Declarations which inaugurated the American and French Revolutions.

The sacred and the civil

The Enlightenment's contributions to the historical understanding of religion and to arguments for toleration confirm that it was far from simply antagonistic towards religion. By contrast, a more direct challenge to ecclesiastical power might seem to lie in 18th-century reflection on the political relation between the civil and the sacred. Here too, however, the issue already had a long history. It had been a preoccupation of Christian thinkers ever since the acceptance of Christianity as the principal religion of the Roman Empire following the conversion of Constantine in 312 AD. If early Christian and medieval thinking had oscillated between endorsement of the connection and an impulse to separate the earthly from the heavenly, the Reformation ensured that the support of the civil powers once again became indispensable to both Protestants and Roman Catholics. In return, rulers developed fresh arguments to keep the churches from encroaching on civil authority.

On the Protestant side, a 16th-century Swiss clergyman, Thomas Erastus, gave his name to a tendency, Erastianism, which held that coercive authority in matters ecclesiastical lay with the civil magistrate alone. The Church of England offered what many believed to be a *sui generis* version of this tendency; and there was a clear sense in which Hobbes only gave it more radical expression. A comparable if more defensive tendency was evident in the Roman Catholic world, in the form of the 'Gallicanism' to which the French monarchy appealed when it wished to confront Papal authority. More generally, Catholic states relied on their civil lawyers to provide them with 'jurisdictionalist' defences against unwanted clerical pretensions to autonomy from civil courts and taxation.

As with toleration, the late 17th century provided a new context in which to restate and develop these arguments. On all sides, civil authorities were determined to avoid a return to religious war, civil or international. Never again should the claims of grace endanger the peace of society, or clergy contest the authority by which the magistrate secured that peace.

One manifestation of this attitude was a new interest in writing 'civil' histories of the states of Europe. Exemplary of these was Pietro Giannone's *Storia civile del regno di Napoli* (1723), a work which, unlike the *Triregno*, he succeeded in publishing (Figure 6). Reconstructing the constitution of the Kingdom of Naples through a history of its laws, Giannone repudiated the claims of the Papacy to be its overlord, and exposed the repeated attempts by ecclesiastical institutions to secure autonomy from the jurisdiction of the crown. Although the reaction of the Church brought Giannone exile and imprisonment, translation of the history into English and French secured his reputation, and made his work a model to later Enlightenment historians.

One of Giannone's admirers was Edward Gibbon (1737–94), whose *Decline and Fall of the Roman Empire* (1776–88) (Figure 7) went back to the root of the problem of the relation between the sacred and the civil. Gibbon began his account of the role of Christianity in the history of the Empire at the conversion of

6. **Pietro Giannone (1676–1748). Frontispiece to the French translation of his *Civil History of the Kingdom of Naples* (1742). Giannone was a Neapolitan historian and fierce critic of the Church, which eventually succeeded in having him imprisoned. Originally published in Italian in 1723, the work was translated into English (in 1729) and French.**

Constantine. Before proceeding with his narrative, however, he decided to end volume 1 (published alone in 1776) with two chapters in which he would explain the causes of the rise of Christianity, and assess the persecutions which Christians had suffered under Constantine's predecessors.

Notoriously, he began the first of these (chapter 15) by stating that he would limit himself to the 'secondary causes' of Christianity's growth, setting aside 'the convincing evidence of the doctrine itself, and the ruling providence of its great Author'. The result was that the chapters were read, whatever Gibbon's intention, as attacks on Christianity: on its Jewish inheritance, the doctrine of the immortal soul, the ambition of its clergy, and the credibility of the numbers and motives of its martyrs. The ferocity of the

THE

HISTORY

OF THE

DECLINE AND FALL

OF THE

ROMAN EMPIRE.

By EDWARD GIBBON, Esq;

VOLUME THE FIRST.

Jam provideo animo, velut qui, proximis littori vadis inducti, mare pedibus ingredi-
untur, quicquid progredior, in vastiorem me altitudinem, ac velut profundum invehi ; et
crescere pene opus, quod prima quæque perficiendo minui videbatur.

LONDON:

PRINTED FOR W. STRAHAN; AND T. CADELL, IN THE STRAND.

MDCCLXXVI.

7. Edward Gibbon's *Decline and Fall of the Roman Empire*. Title page
of volume 1, published in London by W. Strahan and T. Cadell (1776).
Two more volumes were published in 1781, and the final three in 1788.

reaction, even from mild-mannered Anglicans, seems to have surprised Gibbon (though not his friend David Hume)—and when he resumed the narrative in volume 2, his approach changed.

The account he gave in chapter 21 of the great controversy over the Trinity was still charged with irony—at times it is very funny—but it showed a new respect for doctrine. He seems to have realized that to write the history of the Church, which to Christians was sacred history, he must acknowledge that the Church was itself a theological concept. It was impossible, in other words, to write a purely civil history of the relation between the Church and the Empire, between sacred and civil. Gibbon's ambition had become greater: to write a history which did justice to both.

But Gibbon did not confine his engagement with the sacred to Christianity. When he characterized the fall of the Roman Empire as 'the triumph of barbarism and religion' (a phrase borrowed from Voltaire), he had in mind Islam as well as Christianity. He turned to Islam in chapter 50 of the *Decline and Fall*, published in 1788. As in writing the history of Christianity, Gibbon availed himself of the most up-to-date European scholarship, including the results of the Danish expedition to Arabia. As before, he also indulged his taste for irony—and his sense of fun: the Prophet's manliness is duly saluted. But Gibbon took Islam seriously, both as a social and as a religious phenomenon. In its origins it was a religion of the desert, of its *entrepôt* cities, Mecca and Medina, and of its pastoral, Bedouin peoples—a setting much less familiar to Enlightenment historians than either the Americas or East Asia. It was also a distinctive monotheism, whose strength lay in its strict unitarianism.

As Gibbon noted, Mahomet was likely to have been inspired by the Judaism and Christianity he encountered as a young man in Mecca. But he had stripped the idea of God of the metaphysical complexity which made possible Christian doctrines such as the Trinity. As important, he composed in the Koran a sacred text whose incoherence defied rational exposition or historical criticism. In these ways, he had pre-empted the development of a separate order of clergy, whose higher knowledge gave them the spiritual and temporal ambition to challenge the civil power. With its simple injunctions to prayer, fasting, and alms-giving, Islam was a single religious and moral code, accessible to all and offering those who followed its precepts the predestined prospect of eternal pleasure. (In other words, it dispensed with the Christian distinction between a natural law of morality and salvation by divine grace, and elided the civil and the sacred.) Such a monotheism possessed many of the dangerous attributes of 'enthusiasm', the more so once Mahomet directed it towards conquest of the infidel. But it was not an intolerant monotheism like Christianity, for as Gibbon observed in a note, 'the passages in the Koran in behalf of toleration, are strong and numerous'.

In this willingness to engage with the beliefs of Christians and Muslims, rather than simply dismiss them as nonsense or imposture, Gibbon's *Decline and Fall* was emblematic of the best of the Enlightenment's engagement with religion. Certainly, philosophers and historians who identified with Enlightenment were hostile to clerical pretension, intolerance, and doctrinal obscurantism, to superstition and enthusiasm. A few, like Hume, went further, exposing the incoherence of religious truth claims and arguing that Christian moral precepts contradicted the values needed for sociable living. But the interest which Gibbon and many others showed in religion, in its natural, civil, and revealed histories, was not purely critical. Theirs was a major contribution to the understanding of religious doctrine and practice, and of the conditions under which they may be pursued in this world without threatening the peace of society and others' freedom of belief. In these ways, Enlightenment thinkers may also be seen as contributing to the longer-term process of secularization. But they did so not by an attack on religion in general, or on Christianity (or Islam) in particular, but by sceptical, historical enquiry, focused on religion here on earth.

Chapter 3
Bettering the human condition

In his first book, the *Theory of Moral Sentiments* (1759), Adam
Smith (1723–90) posed the question: 'What are the advantages
which we propose by that great purpose of human life which we
call bettering our condition?'

His answer may now come as a surprise: 'To be observed, to be
attended to, to be taken notice of with sympathy, complacency,
and approbation, are all the advantages which we can propose to
derive from it. It is the vanity, not the ease, or the pleasure, which
interests us.'

Smith was not the first to write of human beings' desire to better
their condition. In 1728, in the second volume of his *Fable of the
Bees*, the Dutch philosopher Bernard Mandeville (1670–1733)
identified man's 'perpetual desire of meliorating his condition' as
the cause of his sociableness. Like Adam Smith, Mandeville did
not think this desire was limited to material goods. Instead, he
drew a distinction between our 'self-love', which leads us to seek
the goods necessary to our preservation, and our 'self-liking',
which drives us to try to improve our condition relative to that of
others. In this perspective, bettering our condition requires access
to material goods. But the measure of success is not the possession
of material goods themselves, so much as the acquisition of status,
putting oneself in a position to be admired by others. Neither

Mandeville nor Smith meant to indicate disapproval of the desire to better our condition—on the contrary. But they recognized that the effort would exacerbate inequality in society, and would never be without moral ambivalence.

In this chapter, I shall explore the theme of human betterment in the moral philosophy, history, and political economy of the 18th century. It is in these fields, through intensive enquiry into the motives, causes, and prospects of human betterment, that the greatest originality of Enlightenment thought is to be found. At the heart of the enquiry was the concept of society: why we are, or have become, sociable, and how societies have developed in history.

We shall see that moral ambivalence was built into the enquiry; more than that, the most original single contribution to Enlightenment thinking, by Jean-Jacques Rousseau, was a searing critique of the moral and political consequences of the pursuit of betterment at the expense of others. Nevertheless, there was a response to that critique which, without denying those potentially adverse consequences, demonstrated that betterment of our condition offered mankind a great good: the prospect of freedom from hunger, and a distribution to all ranks of society of a share of the 'necessaries and conveniences' of life. The response came in the form of political economy, and its greatest exponent was Adam Smith, author of the *Wealth of Nations* (1776) (Figure 8).

Moral philosophy and sociability

The prevailing language of moral philosophy in Europe before the 18th century was that of natural law. Until the mid-17th century, its finest exponents were the Catholic philosophers of the 'Second Scholastic', reworking the legacy of Thomas Aquinas. Protestants, meanwhile, adapted natural law to their different theological premises, with a distinctive emphasis on the obligation to seek the

8. 'The Author of the Wealth of Nations', Adam Smith (1790), by John Kay (1742–1826), who drew caricatures of all the major figures of the later Scottish Enlightenment.

good of others. Why Catholic, Scholastic natural law should have fallen away so quickly after 1650 is still unclear. But it seems that its interest in questions of agency and freedom of the will facilitated an increasing focus on casuistry—on the giving of guidance on specific moral issues concerning individual behaviour.

Over the same period, Protestant natural law was transformed by two major interventions. The first was that of Hugo Grotius, whose *De Jure Belli ac Pacis* (1625) adapted the concept of 'right' developed by Catholic jurists to reframe the injunction to respect others as the outcome of a contractual agreement. The second was that of Hobbes, whose *De cive* attacked head on the Aristotelian thesis that man is naturally sociable, and concluded that peace between men could only be achieved through their laying down their natural right, and accepting the authority of an absolute sovereign power. Hobbes's argument was that men are creatures of their passions; the resulting natural unsociability of humans is such that it is meaningless to suggest they ought positively to seek the good of others. It was to this Hobbesian challenge that natural law thinkers subsequently had to respond, and many did so by returning to Grotius for the concepts which would enable them to reconstruct an obligation to sociability.

One of the first to respond, and who in doing so set the agenda of Protestant natural jurisprudence well into the 18th century, was the German philosopher, Samuel Pufendorf (1632–94). Pufendorf's major work was the *De jure naturae et gentium* (1672), his most influential the manual he derived from it for teaching purposes, the *De officio hominis et civis* (1673), *On the Duty of Man and Citizen*.

For Pufendorf the law of nature obliged men to be sociable towards each other by divine command. But he also effectively admitted the thesis of natural unsociability, characterizing the natural state of man in Hobbesian terms as 'a reign of the passions'. Pufendorf's solution to this problem differed from those of Grotius and Hobbes in postponing recourse to the idea of a contract as the device by which men accepted authority. Instead, Pufendorf suggested that there had been an intermediate stage of *socialitas* (sociability) before men entered the *civitas* (the city). Men and women had come together in this intermediate stage despite their suspicion, out of mutual need or 'utility'. Man was not naturally sociable, but had become so in time: the problem of sociability had been solved historically, as men became aware of the law of nature, before there was agreement on the institution of the state.

Pufendorf's conception of natural law was taken up by Christian Thomasius (1655–1728), who made it central to his teaching at the new University of Halle, in Prussia (founded 1694). Thomasius reiterated a version of the thesis of natural unsociability, and of the argument that the antisocial passions had gradually been contained by a culture of 'decorum': the law of nature was God's will, but it was learned by men over time. Thomasius added that the specific purpose of the state was to secure this containment of the passions, above all the religious passions.

The Pufendorfian account of man's acquisition of the natural law of sociability was challenged by Leibniz, who reaffirmed a conception of the law of nature as knowable by human reason, through its participation in God's essential goodness; here, as in metaphysics, he was followed by Christian Wolff. But the dominant tendency in 18th-century German Protestant natural law thinking derived from Pufendorf and Thomasius. Underpinned by an explicitly 'eclectic' attitude to the history of philosophy, Pufendorfian natural law informed teaching not only at Halle but at the increasingly important new university of Göttingen, in Hanover (founded 1737), and indeed throughout Protestant northern Europe.

A different, more Grotian response to Hobbes was offered by John Locke in his *Two Treatises of Government* (1690). Locke accepted that by God's command we are under a direct obligation in natural law to seek the good of others as well as ourselves, under pain of sanction in the life to come. He also held that society and government should be understood as created by contract. But despite affirming that 'an argument from what has been, to what should of right be, has no great force', Locke still acknowledged a historical dimension to the emergence of society, drawing his evidence both from sacred history and from recently discovered America. 'In the beginning'—he famously remarked—'all the world was America'. Since then, however, society had been transformed (and the native inhabitants of America left behind) by the introduction of property in land and the invention of money to allow the accumulation of wealth. These innovations, occurring in time, had necessitated the contract of government.

Outside Germany, Locke's attempted revision of Pufendorf's arguments was variously received and absorbed. One who attempted a synthesis was Gershom Carmichael (1672–1729), regent and subsequently first Professor of Moral Philosophy at the University of Glasgow. But it was the Lausannois Jean Barbeyrac (1674–1744) who did most to consolidate Protestant natural jurisprudence in the early 18th century, editing and annotating the works of all the major authors in the canon, and writing one of the most widely read 'Histories' of moral philosophy as natural law.

In the Catholic intellectual world, meanwhile, the problem of sociability came to the fore by another route. The catalyst was the *Lettres Provinciales* (1657) by Blaise Pascal (1623–62). Inspired by rigorist Augustinian theology, the *Provinciales* were a scathingly ironic attack on the moral casuistry and missionary compromises of the Jesuits. Insisting on the passion-driven concupiscence of fallen man, Pascal effectively denied the capacity of natural law, or of its ancient philosophical progenitor, Stoicism, to render and keep men sociable. But if the Fall had made natural sociability impossible, how then did men manage to live in societies? Pascal and his fellow Augustinian Pierre Nicole could only suppose that self-interest somehow brought and kept humans together. The rising appeal of this Augustinian moral theology coincided with a new interest in Epicurean philosophy as the ancient alternative to Stoicism; in the Epicurean perspective, what was useful and agreeable, rather than a striving for moral excellence, was seen as the best basis for living sociably. But as Pascal and Nicole acknowledged, such worldliness was inseparable from the exercise of deceit in one's relations with others.

The Augustinian perspective resonated in the Protestant world too, in the social commentary of Bernard Mandeville. Mandeville's inspiration was the greatest and most modern of cities: London. At one level, the *Fable of the Bees* (1714, enlarged in 1723) was a satire, an exposure of the hypocrisy of those who would 'reform' the manners of the capital by imposing moral restraint. More profoundly, however, it was, as Mandeville insisted, a work of philosophy, an analysis of the workings of modern sociability.

At the outset, he accepted, men's unsocial passions had only been tamed by the Hobbesian device of the institution of a system of justice. But in a city like London such a framework still gave ample scope for the indulgence of the passions, by both men and women. Mandeville was particularly interested in the role of women as consumers of luxury and arbiters of fashion; in the city, unlike the country, it was possible for those of even moderate means to dress in such a way as to persuade those around them they were of a higher status. Mandeville underlined the economic benefits of luxury consumption: it created employment, encouraged commerce, and promoted diversity. It was a system in which hypocrisy was indeed inevitable; but the benefits, in terms of wealth distribution and individual self-esteem, outweighed the alleged moral costs. Mandeville was in no doubt that London represented betterment of the human condition.

Nevertheless, his argument was provocative rather than persuasive. For not only did it ridicule conventional Christian morality, it failed to provide any coherent moral justification for the behaviour it celebrated. An effort to provide such a justification, however, was the preoccupation of a succession of English, Irish, and Scottish philosophers of the early and mid-18th century. Those critical of Mandeville looked back to the Earl of Shaftesbury (1671–1713), author of the *Characteristics of Men, Manners, Opinions, Times* (1711). Shaftesbury attacked both Hobbes's thesis of natural unsociability and Locke's contention that morality could invoke the sanction of the afterlife. Instead, he offered an idea of morality as a code of manners, natural in that it was based on Stoic principles, but setting a standard of behaviour which could only be sustained by a gentleman with leisure to devote himself to its attainment.

Inspired by Shaftesbury, the Irish Presbyterian philosopher Frances Hutcheson (1694–1746) made a fresh attempt to state the case for natural sociability, and at the same time identify a morality more appropriate to modern society. For Hutcheson, morality, like taste, must be understood to derive from sentiment: specifically, in the case of the former, from a 'moral sense' which naturally suggested benevolence towards others.

Moving from Dublin to Glasgow to succeed Carmichael in the chair of moral philosophy in 1730, Hutcheson devoted his inaugural lecture to a treatment of the problem of sociability, attacking the Epicureanism of Hobbes and Pufendorf, and arguing that natural social affections were the precondition of entering civil society. Hutcheson attributed such natural affections to God's ordering of the world, but invoked the sanction of the afterlife only as an additional inducement to moral culture. As stricter Scottish Presbyterians suspected, he had little stomach for a morality predicated on future rewards and punishments, such as Locke had striven to uphold.

A far more thoroughgoing response to Mandeville, and one which had no recourse whatever to God, was offered by David Hume, initially in the second and third books of his *Treatise of Human*

Nature (1739–40), and subsequently in the *Enquiry Concerning Morals* (1751). Hume allowed that men and women possess some natural abilities and virtues, including a limited benevolence towards those with whom we are connected by family and friendship. These are qualities which are immediately useful and agreeable to those affected. Even so, Hume explained their acceptance as a result of a process of 'sympathy': 'we commonly consider ourselves as we appear in the eyes of others, and sympathize with the advantageous sentiments they entertain with regard to us'. Even the natural virtues are recognized as such only through a process of sympathetic observation.

Hume further insisted that the virtue of justice, on which depend property and government—institutions essential for society—was not natural in this immediate sense. Justice was an artificial virtue, a human convention. This did not mean that it was the outcome of an original, one-off contract, a supposition conceptually incoherent and historically implausible. Justice was an artifice because it could only have been agreed and recognized by a sufficient number of people over time. Hume was prepared to call justice, so achieved, a 'law of nature', but it was natural because it was sanctioned by time. With no reference at all to a divine ordering of the world, Hume had put sociability and the cultivation of morality on a strictly temporal foundation.

A different, less explicitly temporal version of the same general theory of morals was what Adam Smith offered in the *Theory of Moral Sentiments*. Smith began from the principle of 'sympathy', as the common human quality which enables us to enter into the motives and reactions of others, to observe them as spectators, and thence to reach moral judgements on the propriety and utility of their actions. Assuming that society was already advanced in inequality and in the variety of situations in which moral behaviour was expected, Smith went further than Hume in exploring the sheer complexity of our moral judgements. It was thus that he explained our approval for those who better their condition at the expense of ourselves; we still admire and seek to emulate them, and in doing so help to maintain the fabric of society.

Smith did, however, increasingly question whether the vantage point of the ordinary spectator was capable of achieving the highest level of moral judgement. Later editions of the *Moral Sentiments*, culminating in the sixth, published in the year of Smith's death in 1790, introduced and developed the idea of the 'impartial spectator', one better informed of the circumstances in which actions occurred, and less likely to be swayed by the views of the common spectator. But even with this qualification, Smith continued to base his account of morals on the sentiments, not reason, and to assume that the moral sentiments had become more refined over time.

Smith's admission that sympathy with others' motives and circumstances might not be a sufficient basis for a convincing moral philosophy proved to be prescient. For this was precisely the objection advanced by Immanuel Kant: considering ourselves 'as we appear in the eyes of others', as Hume thought we do, was simply not an adequate foundation for morals. Instead of deriving morals from the historical observation of social behaviour, Kant insisted that truly moral principles must be formulated *a priori*, and understood as willed by reason. In this way, he argued in the famously abstract *Groundwork of the Metaphysics of Morals* (1785), a principle of morals would be based on the universal formula of the 'categorical imperative': *act in accordance with a maxim that can at the same time make itself a universal law*. Kant thus returned to the principle of natural law—that a moral value must be of universal application—but did so without assuming a divine command, rational apprehension of the divine ordering of the world, or any basis in human agreement or observable consensus. His rehabilitation of reason in morals owed something to the tradition of Wolffian metaphysics, but Kant insisted on the novelty of his philosophy, differentiating it from all predecessors, whether the natural lawyers or the British exponents of a moral philosophy based in the sentiments and the judgements of spectators.

Individual moral autonomy provided the basis for the public application of reason which Kant offered as the answer to the question 'What is Enlightenment?' The force of Kant's critique of his predecessors has made it tempting to take him at his word, and to identify his philosophy as the culmination of Enlightenment thinking about morals, even as constituting Enlightenment moral philosophy by itself. To foreshorten 18th-century moral enquiry in this way is not simply unhistorical, however; it overlooks the fact that Kant's *a priori* ethics had not resolved the problem of sociability. To the contrary, Kant acknowledged the problem's intractability by reformulating it himself as that of 'unsocial sociability'. In doing so he accepted that it was a problem in human history, where the prevalence of the passions, what he called the 'crooked timber' of humanity, meant that the prospects of men and women abiding by the rule of the categorical imperative were limited or even non-existent, now and for the foreseeable future.

In his essay 'Idea for a universal history with a cosmopolitan purpose' (1784), Kant suggested that if mankind were to reinstate the idea that a 'Providence' gives purpose to human existence, it would be possible to envisage, at least in principle, the gradual acceptance of the standard of the categorical imperative, and hence the achievement of truly moral sociability. As we shall see, however, the assumption of a purpose to history was one that other Enlightenment historians and philosophers of history overwhelmingly repudiated. Even if mankind could be said to have overcome its original or natural unsociability through history, the same history offered little prospect of a lasting solution to human rivalry and conflict. What it did hold, nevertheless, was a real prospect of material human betterment.

History

The turn to history associated with the Enlightenment is exemplified (though not exhausted) by the great panoramic narratives of Voltaire, Hume, Robertson, and Gibbon. These were not simply narratives in the tradition of the Renaissance masters, Machiavelli and Guicciardini. Rather, they were avowedly 'philosophical', in that they were set within an extended analytical perspective.

The Enlightenment historians believed that political events should be understood in the framework of the 'society' within which they took place. The historian should attend to social structure—the distribution of ranks—and also to the 'manners' of a people; he or she should also be aware of the constraints placed upon nations by their geographic location, climate, and means of economic subsistence. These factors had not been ignored before the 18th century; ever since the discovery of hitherto unknown continents and peoples in the 16th century, writers on the 'art of history' had urged its practitioners to incorporate them. But it was a challenge which had hitherto proved beyond European historians; it was only in the 18th century that it was taken up, to become a distinctive attribute of Enlightenment historical writing.

The work which more than any other inspired Enlightenment historians to think in this way was the *Esprit des lois* (*The Spirit of the Laws*) (1748), by Charles Louis, Baron de Montesquieu (1689-1755). This was not itself a work of history, except in its final books devoted to the history of feudal law in France. It was a study of forms of government, classified by Montesquieu into three basic types:—republics, monarchies, and despotisms—and analysed in relation to their distinctive values, prevailing manners, geographical situation, climate, and economic aptitudes. All these must be considered, Montesquieu argued, if we are to understand the 'spirit' of a nation's laws and constitution. The implicit contrast was with the juristic perspective of the natural and civil lawyers, which Montesquieu set aside in favour of the comparative and historical study of government in the full range of its possible settings.

At the core of *The Spirit of the Laws* was a comparison between the mixed, republican-monarchic government of England and the absolute monarchy of France—a comparison by no means to the latter's disadvantage. But what distinguished the work was its inclusiveness, its author's reluctance to wield Occam's razor: very little was beyond his curiosity. Many readers, among them Hume and Gibbon, might find the laconic, aphoristic style of the work irritating, but Montesquieu transformed how politics was understood and history written as no author had done since Machiavelli.

To this comparative perspective 18th-century historians added something more: for the first time, history was conceived of as a dynamic process, as 'progress'. As we shall see, Enlightenment historians did not think of progress as unambiguously positive—far from it. But they did think that societies developed—that it was possible therefore to think in terms of 'the progress of society'.

To do this, they went back to the beginning, to identify what appeared to be the earliest phases of social existence. As we saw in Chapter 2, sacred history was one invaluable source of information on the first men and their families. Another was the Americas: both the peoples discovered and conquered by the Spanish, and the still independent native peoples of North America with whom British, French, and Dutch colonists were attempting (unequally) to share the land. Behind Locke's observation that 'in the beginning, all the world was America' lay volumes of travellers' and missionaries' reports, including the remarkable *Natural and Moral History of the East and West Indies* (1590) by the Spanish Jesuit, José de Acosta. Acosta had recognized that it was not enough to cast the various peoples of the Americas together as 'barbarous'. Some were indeed at that level: nomadic, loosely grouped, constantly at war. But others had formed communities, which cultivated the earth and possessed property. Following Locke, the 18th-century historians inferred that these were the preconditions of progress.

A second, more recently available source for the study of the earliest men and women was the comparative anatomy of the animals thought to be closest to man, the apes and the 'orang-outang'. In an influential study of 1699, the English naturalist Edward Tyson had represented the 'orang-outang' (actually a young chimpanzee) as capable of walking on its hind legs and possessing organs of speech; subsequently both the Swedish naturalist Linnaeus and the French natural historian Buffon had produced new series of types of man, blurring the difference between human and animal, and offering new insights into the acquisition of practical skills as well as language.

It was a possible consequence of such thinking, however, that as the difference between man and animal diminished, the difference between types of human might increase, with the white European at one (the higher) end of the spectrum, the black African at the other, closest to the supposed 'orang-outang'. Reinforcing that hypothesis was the heterodox thought, first canvassed in the mid-17th century, that Adam had not, after all, been the very first man: for his son, Cain, to have found a wife, there must have been others in the world before Adam. In other words, the origins of the peoples of the world had been polygenetic, not monogenetic. Such a claim was attractive to religious sceptics such as Voltaire and Hume; combined with the naturalists' differentiation of types of human, it permitted what appears to be a straightforward racial hierarchy. Such ideas lay behind Hume's now notorious footnote remark that he was 'apt to suspect the negroes, and in general all the other species of men (for there are four or five different kinds) to be naturally inferior to the whites'. From here to a defence of black slavery might be but a further, short step—though it should be emphasized that it was not one taken by Hume, who denounced the slavery practiced in the ancient world.

For Enlightenment historians, however, the critical question was not whether there were natural, racial differences between humans, but why some human societies, above all those of Europe, had been able to develop, while others, those of native Americans and Africans, now lagged so far behind. The explanation was found in an explicitly stadial theory of social development. The stages were variously characterized: some historians continued to work with the classical categories of 'savage', 'barbarian', and 'civilized' (the last deriving from the *civis*, the city). Adam Ferguson (1723–1816), Scottish author of *An Essay on the History of Civil Society* (1767), distinguished savage from barbarian societies by the latter's acceptance of property; but it was only in 'polished and commercial nations' that the personal rights of the individual were fully secured within a hierarchy of social and political 'subordination'. More original was the classification of stages according to the prevailing mode of subsistence: in fully developed form, this was a 'four-stages theory', of hunting, pastoral, agricultural, and commercial societies.

The idea that there were successive modes of subsistence was not the same as the later Marxist concept of modes of production: even so, what interested Enlightenment historians were the ways in which the different modes of subsistence corresponded with different property arrangements, variety of manners, distinct roles for women, and different systems of authority. Telling use of the theory was made by William Robertson (1721–93) in his *History of America* (1777), a study of the conquest and colonization of both South and North America; but the classic exposition was to be found in Adam Smith's *Wealth of Nations*, where it was combined with a model of the 'natural progress of opulence' from agriculture to commerce. Using stadial theory enabled historians to think explicitly in terms of the 'progress of society', but this did not mean that movement from one stage to the next would be automatic (especially in the earliest stages), and it carried no connotation of teleology, of inherently purposive development. As Kant realized, that required separate philosophical justification, in which Enlightenment historians generally showed little interest.

While the material circumstances of a society provided stadial history with its base, Enlightenment historians were at least as interested in the different 'manners' or 'moeurs' of the societies they studied. Montesquieu made moeurs central to the spirit of a nation's laws, while Voltaire entitled his universal history an *Essai sur les moeurs* (1755). Without using the word in their titles, Hume, Robertson, and Gibbon all sought to show that manners were integral to the explanation of nations' differing fortunes. Two aspects of this interest merit more attention.

One is the interest in the origin of language. In one guise, this was a technical question in the philosophy of knowledge: if all knowledge derived from the senses, as Locke argued and the editors of the *Encyclopédie* agreed, how, and how well, do words represent what the senses present to human understanding? The question was addressed by Condillac in his *Essay on the Origin of Human Knowledge* (1746), and continued to be debated across Europe, not least at the Berlin Academy of Sciences, refounded by Frederick II of Prussia.

But the debate, in Berlin and elsewhere, was also framed historically, as a series of questions about the circumstances in which men and women would first have needed to communicate, what their primitive communications would naturally have consisted in, and how more sophisticated languages might subsequently have developed. These questions were increasingly answered by conjectural, naturalistic histories of language; a notable example was the account offered by Mandeville in volume 2 of the *Fable of the Bees*. But such histories raised a difficulty of their own: if language was indispensable to society, did it not have to exist already? This left an opening for those who continued to insist that language was one of God's gifts to man.

As interesting to historians as its origins, however, was the continuing role of language in the evolution and civilizing of a nation's manners. This would be manifest not only in its literature, but in its political oratory, and in more personal forms of communication; in letters and conversation—'commerce' in its broadest social sense. A civilized society would be distinguished by the sophistication of its language use, and by the good manners which it fostered.

An important measure of that sophistication, and a second noteworthy subject of the history of manners, was the condition of women. Women were now the explicit subjects of histories: in French, the *Essai sur le caractère, les moeurs et l'esprit des femmes* (1772) by Antoine-Léonard Thomas, in English *The History of Women from the Earliest Antiquity* (1779), by William Alexander; they were likewise given a substantial place in John Millar's *Observations concerning the Distinction of Ranks in Society* (1771). Among histories by women were the *History of England* (1763–83) by the radical Catherine Macaulay (1731–91), and the multi-volume *Histoire d'Elisabeth, reine d'Angleterre* (1786–9) by Louise de Kéralio (1758–1821).

For all this, however, the degree of agency to be attributed to women in history remained unclear. Most historians who utilized the stadial model of development were confident that the condition of women had improved with the progress of society. Abused in early, savage societies, women were accorded much more respect, and in return demanded better manners of men in refined and civilized societies. The implications of the idea and practice of chivalry for women received particular attention, even if the historians divided over its merits. But agency—the ability to change the course of history—was still at a premium. There were queens, both wicked (Mary Queen of Scots) and wise (Elizabeth of

England), while emperors and kings had scheming lovers. But few women below those levels were recognized as individual historical subjects.

The place to be accorded to women was, in fact, a symptom of a more general problem facing Enlightenment historians: how to integrate geography, economic circumstances, and manners into large-scale narratives. The 'philosophic historians' of the Enlightenment struggled to write histories of society and of manners at the same time and in the same work as more conventional histories of government and of relations between rulers. They were perhaps most successful in integrating the history of religion into their narratives. By contrast, economic history, social manners, and the history of literature tended to be treated as asides, or, as in Hume's *History*, relegated to appendices. But the philosophic historians were hardly unique in this failure; the problem of combining narrative with structural explanation was no better resolved in the 19th and 20th centuries, and continues to frustrate the modern scholarly historian. The achievement of the Enlightenment historians was to be the first to conceptualize the problem and to address it in their compositions. Even if they failed, they left some of the finest histories ever written, and in Gibbon's *Decline and Fall of the Roman Empire*, one unmatched in any age in its sweep, interpretative ambition, and grandeur of style. So doing, they placed a historical perspective, a conviction of the 'progress of society', at the heart of Enlightenment thought.

Rousseau

Within the Enlightenment, one thinker held out against the view that history is a progress of society—and powerfully reinforced the sense of ambivalence over the morals of the modern commercial age: Jean-Jacques Rousseau (1712–78) (Figure 9). He had first made his name as a critic of the arts and sciences—of luxury—and the range of his writing was wide: music (including the composition

9. Jean-Jacques Rousseau. Portrait by Maurice Quentin de la Tour (1753). A portrait of a forty-year-old Rousseau, by which time he was known for his prize-winning *Discourse on the Arts and Sciences* (1751), and for his jaunty opera, *The Village Fortune-teller* (1752). His greatest works were still to come.

of an opera, *Le Devin du Village*, 1752), moral and political philosophy (the *Contrat Social*, 1762), education (*Emile*, also 1762), an epistolary novel (*Julie, ou la nouvelle Héloïse*, 1761), and autobiographical confessions (published after his death, in 1782).

But it was his engagement with the moral and historical question of sociability, its origins and consequences, in his *Discours sur l'origine et les fondements de l'inégalité parmi les homes* (1755), often known as the 'Second Discourse', which had the greatest impact on his fellow philosophers. The work was composed in 1754, as an answer to the question, posed by the Academy of Dijon: 'What is the origin of inequality among men, and is it authorized by natural law?'

Rousseau set aside the second part of the question, leaving it to the reader to notice that natural law had no part to play in the answer. Instead he framed the question as one concerning man's natural condition, and his subsequent passage into society. For this purpose, he deliberately stepped outside of the earliest known history, that recounted in the book of Genesis, and conjectured what man's original, natural condition must have been. This, he emphasized, was the kind of conjecture now made by natural philosophers to determine the formation of the world; it was not 'conjectural history' (a term soon to come into use), in that it did not aspire to fill in the gaps in existing evidence.

As Rousseau envisaged them, the earliest men and women were solitary creatures, who roamed alone, gathering food and coupling when they encountered one another. As such, they had indeed been very similar to the 'orang-outang' of Tyson's portrayal. They were naturally self-interested, seeking self-preservation, but they had a repugnance to the suffering of others; 'pity' was a natural sentiment in man, as it seemed to be in animals. It was a condition of natural unsociability, but not one in which individuals were dominated by the selfish passions. What humans did have, and animals did not, was free will, and hence the crucial quality of 'perfectibility', the capacity to change, to improve—or to corrupt—their original condition.

It was only when men and women were forced together by population growth and geographical constraints (oceans, mountain ranges) that their passions became competitive, and the ambiguities of their perfectibility became apparent. They formed settled families, and they acquired language. It was Rousseau who wondered aloud 'Which came first, language or society?'—and hence gave renewed hope to those who wanted language to be innate, or a divine gift.

What he would emphasize, however, was how little nature had done to bring men together, or to facilitate their use of speech;

instinct alone had given man all he needed to live in the state of nature. Once men and women lived together in society, however, language acquired all too much potency. It played a critical role in the decisive moment of transition, the establishment of property. This occurred when men began to specialize, one to cultivate the ground, another to make the tools required by the cultivator. At that point it became in the cultivator's interest to claim exclusive ownership of the land he cultivated. But the claim alone did not make it property; it was the acceptance of the claim by others which was decisive. That acceptance was the result of the persuasive power of language. And in accepting the institution of property, men and women agreed to inequality, to society organized hierarchically and divisively.

The establishment of inequality through the institution of property had two devastating consequences. The first was to exacerbate the split within the human passion of self-love, cleaving *amour propre* from simple *amour de soi*, and encouraging humans to distinguish themselves from their fellows, to show themselves to be unequal. As Pascal and Mandeville had already suggested, pride of this sort could only be maintained by deceit; but where they had seen social utility, Rousseau saw only degradation: 'to be and to appear became two totally different things, and from this distinction arose ostentatious display, deceitful cunning, and all the vices that follow in their wake'.

The second consequence was the predominance of the city over the countryside. The agriculturalist may have won the race for property in the land, but increasingly he was lured to squander his surplus on goods produced in the city, as the division of labour enabled its inhabitants to specialize in the manufacture of inessential luxuries. Falling into debt, many farmers abandoned their land to migrate to the city; and there the sheer concentration of humanity facilitated the consolidation of ever more despotic forms of government.

By now, Rousseau's was an explicitly historical argument, an outline of the essential course of modern European history. But his was a history with a very different *dénouement* to that envisaged by exponents of the 'progress of society'. For Rousseau explicitly identified modern civilization with corruption. He made the point by a final dramatic comparison between savage and civilized man. The savage 'breathes nothing but repose and freedom'; he lives 'within himself'. The citizen, by contrast, 'forever active, sweats, scurries, constantly agonizes in search of ever more strenuous occupations . . . He courts the great whom he hates, and the rich whom he despises.' He 'is capable of living only in the opinion of others'. This was a critique far more thoroughgoing than the traditional lament of classically inspired moralism. Corruption as Rousseau understood it was so dangerous because it was a process within history, an integral consequence of that 'progress of society' which offered men hitherto unimaginable material rewards and social status. Corruption was but the other face of betterment.

The force of this critique was such that very few Enlightenment philosophers failed to register it and respond. Hume was one of the few, and paid for his misunderstanding when, after a successful visit to Paris between 1763 and 1766, he attempted to befriend Rousseau and bring him to England: the rapid breakdown in their relationship became an international *cause célèbre*. Adam Smith, by contrast, shaped his moral and (as we shall see) economic thinking as an answer to Rousseau. But the latter's impact was felt all over Europe: in Naples, for example, Antonio Genovesi (1713–69) would reconstruct his moral philosophy to defend political economy from Rousseau's attack. In at least one sphere, moreover, the critique was taken up and developed in ways Rousseau may not have foreseen.

For an important but still underappreciated aspect of Enlightenment thinking was its anti-imperialism, manifest in critical treatments of European engagement with other, apparently backward peoples discovered by explorers and missionaries. Inspiration for this attitude was drawn not so much from ideals of 'natural man' or the 'noble savage', such as might be derived from a simplistic reading of Rousseau, as from curiosity about the variety of human culture.

What interested the philosophers was the apparently limitless capacity of peoples to differentiate themselves by their manners. A famous example was the sexual generosity of South Sea Islanders, encountered by the English Captain Cook and the French Captain Bougainville, who had returned with a Tahitian to show off in Paris. The French captain's version of his encounter was the subject of Diderot's biting *Supplément au voyage de Bougainville* (1773–4), in which he exposed the exploitative intent of Bougainville, and set off the sexual freedom of the islanders against the hypocrisy of Christian morals.

But Diderot's critique was most fully developed in the *Histoire des deux Indes* (1770–80). The author of this work was identified as the Abbé Raynal, but his role was as much that of editor; scholars have established that by the 1780 edition, substantial parts of the work had been written by Diderot. It was Diderot, moreover, who gave the work its sharpest tone. The *History of the Two Indies* was not hostile to commerce as such, and even admitted that slavery was a commercial necessity for the Caribbean colonies. But it repeatedly attacked the behaviour of Europeans within their colonies, their treatment of native peoples, and, above all, of their slaves. Another target was the indiscriminate cruelty and economic disruption wrought by European pirates.

If this work by Raynal and Diderot had the greatest impact, its perspective was by no means unique. Adam Smith was a vigorous critic of the monopolistic trading companies which Europeans used to dominate trade, not only between the colonies and Europe, but within the colonial world itself. Kant identified maritime commerce as one of the key causes of war, encouraging aggression towards native peoples and European rivals alike.

Perhaps most disillusioned of all was Herder, for whom travel literature confirmed his conviction that nations and their distinctive cultures were the key to human sociability in all its variety, only to observe those cultures abused and trampled on by European greed and arrogance.

The evils of empire were a relatively marginal part of Rousseau's critique of modern civilization, but the extent to which they were acknowledged in the second half of the 18th century is testimony to Rousseau's impact in questioning the moral consequences of Europe's progress. Rousseau had got under the skin of Enlightenment intellectual optimism, and his criticisms would never be disposed of. He exerted such an impact, however, precisely because he engaged so thoroughly with the central preoccupations of his fellow philosophers; he was by no means exceptional, or external, or 'counter' to Enlightenment.

Political economy

What confirms Rousseau's centrality is that his challenge was answered. None was clearer in doing so, moreover, than Adam Smith. As we have seen, Smith was without illusion in acknowledging that what drove men and women to better their condition was the ambition to acquire status in the eyes of others. At the very end of his life, he positively reinforced this admission, by adding to the sixth edition of the *Theory of Moral Sentiments* a chapter entitled 'Of the corruption of our moral sentiments, which is occasioned by this disposition to admire the rich and the great, and to despise or neglect persons of poor and mean condition'. The impartial spectator of commercial society could not but be ambivalent about its values. But Smith did not withdraw his countervailing contention that it was the drive to better our condition which resulted in material prosperity—for all ranks of society. It may do so as if by 'an invisible hand', as an unintended consequence; but when the rich employ thousands in 'the gratification of their own vain and insatiable desires, they divide with the poor the produce of all their improvements'. To explain why this was so, Smith proceeded to write the *Wealth of Nations*. A landmark in the history of economic thought, the *Wealth of Nations* was also the culmination of the emergence of political economy as a discourse of Enlightenment.

The roots of political economy lie in the 17th century. It was then that the term was coined (in the first instance in French), and that economic activity became the subject of extended commentary as the basis of a nation's standing and power. Early in the century the *arbitristas* debated whether the problems facing the Spanish monarchy may have had something to do with its reliance on American silver. By the mid century the rulers of German states devastated by the Thirty Years War were turning to the new discourse of 'cameralism' to learn how to rebuild their populations and basic economic resources. But the most vigorous debates, in which participants offered markedly different diagnoses of problems and solutions to them, took place in England and in France. Prominent in the English debate were Thomas Mun, Nicholas Barbon, William Petty, Henry Martin, and John Cary. Cary's *Essay on the State of England* (1695) was representative in its concern with the perceived threat from Ireland, whose low labour costs threatened English industries; if England lost competitiveness in manufactures, it was likely to fall under the commercial hegemony of either the Dutch or France. The French were no less anxiously debating their own prospects. Louis XIV's minister Colbert made a strong case for the protection and encouragement of manufactures and merchant shipping to complement France's agricultural resources. Others, opposed to the military aggression of Louis, insisted that agriculture should be put first, and manufacturing, especially of luxuries, curtailed. Boisguilbert argued for the primacy of agriculture in the face of the disproportionate growth of Paris, while Archbishop Fénelon's allegory, *Télémaque* (1699), suggested that urban populations be stripped of their luxuries and forcibly returned to the countryside.

It was in France that the foundations of Enlightenment political economy were laid in the first half of the 18th century. The failure of the Scottish financier John Law's ambitious plan to refinance the French public debt, the 'Mississippi Scheme', in 1720 was the catalyst. His former secretary, Jean-François Melon (1675–1738), offered an analysis of the causes of the failure, placing it within a general account of the workings of a modern economy. Melon's *Essai politique sur le commerce* (1734) was significant at several levels. It supported its arguments with imagined scenarios (in effect, models); it was explicit in its assumption of the primacy of 'utility', to the point of arguing that 'luxury' was a moralistic term best dispensed with (a rebuttal of Fénelon); and it was sufficiently comprehensive in its coverage to serve as a manual. As such, it was to be read across Europe for the remainder of the century, and frequently translated into other languages. In Naples it was seized on by improvers in the early 1740s, and its lasting appeal was marked by translations in 1778 and 1795.

The impact of Melon's work was reinforced in the 1750s by the publications of a circle of economic writers led by Vincent de Gournay (1712–59). Prominent among its members were Butel-Dumont, Forbonnais, and Turgot. Gournay particularly encouraged translations, which in one year, 1755, included Cantillon's *Essai sur la nature du commerce*, Cary's *Essai sur l'état du commerce d'Angleterre*, rewritten as well as translated by Butel-Dumont, and Hume's *Discours politiques*, translated by the Abbé le Blanc. Gournay's initiative was vital in breaching the French monarchy's defensive assumption that the economy, as the basis of royal finances, should be a 'reason of state', withheld from public discussion; but it also spread a much greater volume of economic works across French-speaking Europe.

The keynote of this French political economy was that agriculture was the foundation of a healthy national economy. The premise was that France, like other Mediterranean countries, but unlike the Netherlands, had an abundance of fertile land. The danger in such fertility was that agriculturalists lacked the incentive to increase productivity, rendering the entire nation vulnerable to harvest failures from natural causes. But the danger could be averted by encouraging domestic manufactures, which would offer farmers the incentive to increase their productivity, thus gaining both greater spending power and a reserve against shortages. To encourage both manufactures and the free circulation of grain, internal commerce should be facilitated by investment in communications and the regulation of tolls.

Foreign commerce, by contrast, should be restricted: it was important that those with spending power did not divert their wealth into the purchase of foreign luxuries, compromising the balance within the national economy, and facilitating the excessive growth of its cities, the capital in particular. There were of course differences of emphasis: Melon's dismissal of the bogey of luxury was not shared by others, including Montesquieu. But there was also consensus: both Melon and Gournay accepted that a nation's foreign commerce might have to be regulated.

Subsequently the physiocrats, headed by François Quesnay, reworked the argument for the primacy of agriculture in more analytical terms, and drew out some radical policy consequences. Since the land alone yielded a surplus, it should be the sole source of taxation, and all internal obstacles to the internal movement of grain should be removed. The physiocrats are often thought of as the only French economists worthy of note in the Enlightenment, but this is a mistake. Rather they refined and radicalized a line of argument reaching back through Melon to Boisguilbert. They were, moreover, undermined by successive government failures to impose free trade in grain in the 1760s and 1770s, and by an intellectual backlash led by the Neapolitan economist Ferdinando Galiani, supported by Diderot, calling for a more pragmatic approach.

The influence of French political economy on the development of economic thinking in other Mediterranean countries underlines the mistake of concentrating attention on physiocracy. In Italy the impact of Melon was soon reinforced by the translations undertaken by the Gournay circle. Butel-Dumont's version of Cary's *Essai* was translated again, into Italian as the *Storia del commercio della Gran Bretagna* (1757–8) by Antonio Genovesi, who added his own 'annotations'. Later Genovesi published his own synthesis, the *Lezioni di commercio* (1765–7), which combined the arguments of the French with those of Hume on money, and adapted them to the circumstances of southern Italy. Less derivative were the Milanese economists Cesare Beccaria and Pietro Verri, especially the latter, the most thoughtful of the Italians. But he too engaged primarily with the arguments of the French. In Spain Melon was again a point of reference, translated in 1743 (the first in Europe) and again in 1786. So too was Genovesi, whose *Lezioni* were the subject of two translations in the 1780s.

When physiocratic ideas were added to the discussion, it was in a form which blended them with earlier thinking. The key text in this process was by a Swiss writer, Georg-Ludwig Schmid D'Avenstein, whose *Principes de la législation universelle* (1776) was immediately translated into Italian. Schmid's work was particularly popular in Naples, where a further translation appeared in 1791. In both Italy and Spain, the adaptation of political economy to local circumstances was seen as the key to 'reform' and 'improvement', without which those countries would have no prospect of catching up on the mercantile nations of northern Europe.

Elsewhere, the French model was less persuasive. German economic thinking in the 18th century continued to be dominated by cameralism. Gradually cameralism was incorporated into university curricula, first in Protestant northern Germany, later in the south and in Austria. The first textbooks were written by two Austrians, Johann von Justi and Joseph von Sonnenfels, in 1755 and 1765 respectively, the former's entitled *Staatswirthschaft* (*State Economy*). In time the Germans opened up: physiocratic ideas were discussed in the 1770s, those of Adam Smith in the 1790s, despite an earlier partial translation of the *Wealth of Nations* in 1776–9. Significantly, however, the *Principles of Political Economy* (1767) by Smith's less liberal Scottish contemporary, Sir James Steuart, translated as *Grundsätze der Staatswirthschaft* (1769–70), received more attention than the *Wealth of Nations*. The focus remained on the economic needs of the German states, and on training administrators to respond to them. Late in the century, the idea of the 'national economy' came to the fore, as an explicit defence of German autonomy between the competing ambitions of the French and the British to European economic hegemony.

The most famous national contribution to Enlightenment political economy was that of the Scots, David Hume and Adam Smith; and both framed their arguments as a response to those of the French. The first of Hume's economic essays in the *Political Discourses* (1752), 'Of Commerce', took issue specifically with Melon, while Smith singled out the physiocrats for criticism (but also praise) in the *Wealth of Nations*.

For Hume and Smith it had been commerce, not agriculture, which held the key to Europe's development. There was no separate development path for supposedly 'fertile' countries like France and Italy. Commerce not only made goods available to agricultural producers, offering a necessary incentive to productivity; but by introducing new products from overseas to the domestic market, it gave inspiration and incentive to manufacturers to design new and cheaper products of their own. With that would come an intensifying division of labour and technological innovation. On this basis, Hume argued, commerce benefitted poor countries which could take advantage of their lower wage levels; but this was unlikely to be to the long-run disadvantage of already rich countries, which could respond through the division of labour and innovation. Commerce, international as well as national, was not a zero-sum competition: as 'a British subject', Hume was happy to 'pray for the flourishing commerce of Germany, Spain, Italy, and even France itself'.

Both Scots, however, appreciated that what Hume called 'jealousy of trade' prevailed among European states. In the *Wealth of Nations*, Smith explained this as the historical outcome of an 'unnatural and retrograde' economic order. The 'natural progress of opulence', as Smith understood it, would have seen commerce developing last, after agriculture and manufactures, because returns to capital were greater in these than in either domestic or foreign trade.

In Europe, however, the fall of the Roman Empire to the barbarian invasions had resulted in the transfer of a servile agricultural labour force from one set of masters to another, even more predatory. The new feudal lords had put numbers of retainers before any thought of investment in the land. It was only when tempted by the 'baubles and trinkets' offered to them by overseas merchants that the lords had dismissed their retainers and freed their serfs, who had then moved to the towns to provide manufacturers with a free labour force.

This 'unnatural' process had the beneficial consequence of giving manufacturers and eventually even landowners incentive to invest; but it had also placed merchants, in particular overseas merchants and trading companies, in the driving seat of economic policy. The result was what Smith termed 'the mercantile system', under which merchants persuaded gullible, ignorant governments to favour their particular interests, at the expense of open commerce. Smith, like Hume, was fiercely critical of such 'jealousy of trade': it threatened to make Europe and Europe's global trade a scene of perpetual conflict, driven by the desire to control resources and markets.

Nevertheless, both Hume and Smith were confident of the benefits of commerce to society, at every level. Not only did it ensure that the public would have more resources with which to defend itself,

Hume argued, but individuals, including labourers, would have more of the 'necessaries, or even the chief conveniencies of life' than ever before. Smith explicitly defined the wealth of a nation as its per capita income, and argued that it was the distinguishing feature of a fully commercial society that it increased. Concluding his discussion of property right, Locke had remarked that 'a king of a large and fruitful territory' in the Americas 'feeds, lodges, and is clad worse than a day labourer in England'. Smith repeated this sentiment, now making the comparison with an African king, at the end of the opening chapter of the *Wealth of Nations*—and proceeded to support it with historical and economic explanation which Locke barely anticipated. Only in a commercial society, Hume and Smith argued, are all the people better off, and free from the spectre of harvest failure.

With this, the Scots offered the most powerful of all responses to Rousseau's critique of modern society. In denouncing inequality, and its economic, moral, and political consequences, Rousseau had not denied that society must have an economic base. What he sought was 'balanced' growth between the country and the city—a vision which stopped short of Fénelon's call for the repatriation of city dwellers to the country. What Hume and more fully Smith had demonstrated, however, was that any such 'balance' would be inherently precarious. Only a commitment to commerce, conducted as freely as might be compatible with a nation's defence, would generate the growth which would improve everyone's life for the better. Growth through commerce might have undeniable moral costs, but it still bettered the human condition.

Smith's *Wealth of Nations*, of course, did not settle the argument for ever: there was plenty of dissent among economists in the final decades of the 18th century, let alone in the century to come. French economists continued to seek an answer to British economic supremacy, which they took Smith's arguments to reinforce, before and after the outbreak of the Revolution. In turn, German economists sought to defend themselves from both, and drew on Rousseau's inspiration for the idea of a 'closed commercial state', which would reap the benefits of commerce while protecting domestic producers. What was not now disputed, however, was the transformative power of commerce, and the human industry it released. As the science of commerce, political economy thus became the key to understanding modern society and its prospects of further development; in effect, it became the new universal science of society, occupying the intellectual space once claimed by natural jurisprudence.

Here, I suggest, was the core of the Enlightenment's contribution to Western thought: political economy as the prospect of human betterment, in this world rather than the next, in the present over the past. This was betterment conceived in a historical perspective, the perspective of 'the progress of society'. It was a perspective conscious of its limits: no variant of Enlightenment political economy promised endless growth, to the point of overcoming scarcity or achieving equality of access to wealth and status. Marx's utopian technological vision of all enjoying equal independent leisure was *not* that of Enlightenment historians or political economists. Enlightenment philosophers, historians, and economists were all too well aware of the enduring obstacles to commerce, not least from ill-informed, short-sighted governments. Still, they were optimistic, observing that the activities of a modern commercial economy were so diverse, and required the decisions of so many individuals across the world, that they were now beyond the ability of any government to control. There really were, they believed, 'economic limits to national politics'. This was why Smith famously expressed confidence in the *Wealth of Nations* that:

> The natural effort of every individual to better his condition, when suffered to exert itself with freedom and security, is so powerful a principle, that it is alone, and without any assistance, not only capable of carrying on the society to wealth and prosperity, but of surmounting a hundred impertinent obstructions with which the folly of human laws too often incumbers its operations.

The political corollary of this conviction was that governments should listen to society, and be guided by its 'opinion'. As we shall see in Chapter 4, the conviction that political influence must now be exerted through public opinion distinguished the Enlightenment approach to politics, constituting its novel strength and, in the end, fatal weakness.

Chapter 4
Enlightening the public

Given the intellectual effort which Enlightenment thinkers put into understanding society, the economy, religion, and politics, it is natural for historians to ask what impact they had on their own societies—how successful they were in promoting the causes with which they were associated.

When historians first began serious study of Enlightenment, in the mid-20th century, their focus was upon the direct political application of Enlightenment ideas. Inevitably this drew them to the relation between Enlightenment and revolution: explanation of the greatest single event of the 18th century, the French Revolution, remains the priority, especially for French historians. But revolution had its antecedents in reform, or, more often, in failed reform, and here Enlightenment thinkers had been involved in larger numbers and at least as directly as they were to be in the Revolution, seeking to influence the policy of rulers, and especially kings and princes.

For this alliance historians coined the phrase 'Enlightened despotism', or, less pejoratively, 'Enlightened absolutism'. The obvious candidates for attention under this heading were the three most prominent rulers of the century, Frederick II of Prussia (ruled 1740 to 1786), Catherine II of Russia (1762–96)—both of whom attracted individual *philosophes* to their courts—and the still more radical Emperor, Joseph II of Austria, Bohemia, and Hungary (who ruled jointly with his mother, Maria Theresia, from 1765 and alone from 1780 to 1790).

Since the 1970s, however, historians' focus has shifted away from the political history of Enlightenment to its social and, most recently, its cultural history. The question of its impact is now considered one of social practice and print culture: institutions of sociability, the publishing industry, and readers now command attention. Yet while much has been learned from research into these subjects, there remains a danger that the cultural history of Enlightenment may submerge the intellectual, by treating the arguments of the philosophers as secondary to the institutions and the media through which they were propagated and received.

In this chapter, I shall outline what historians have revealed of the context in which Enlightenment ideas were formed and received; but I shall argue that what distinguished the Enlightenment was the agency of philosophers and men of letters in relation to their 'public'. What they sought was a new role for themselves as formers of 'public opinion', understood as an instrument by which they could guide but also effectively limit what governments could hope to achieve. At the end I shall return to the classic question of the relation between Enlightenment and revolution, to argue, however, that we should see the Enlightenment as overtaken by the Revolution, and brought to an end by the revolutionary eruption of direct political action.

The 'public sphere'

No concept has done more to shape historical understanding of the Enlightenment's relation to society than that of the 'public sphere'. It was coined by the young German philosopher Jürgen Habermas, in *The Structural Transformation of the Public Sphere*, first published in German in 1962. 'Public sphere' is the term used in the English translation for the German *Öffentlichkeit*, which may also be rendered as 'public' or 'publicity'.

As originally published, the book was a contribution to the philosophical debate over the Enlightenment—a point to whose significance I shall return in Chapter 5. By the time it appeared in English (in 1989, following a French translation in 1978), however, it had also become an inspiration to historians. This was because Habermas, a historical sociologist in the tradition of Marx and Weber, had based his argument on a substantial body of historical evidence from the late 17th and 18th centuries.

The outline of the argument was recognizably Marxist. In 'feudal' society the nobility, the church, and the royal or princely ruler had monopolized 'publicness', controlling its expression in art and in written media. With the advent of capitalist social relations, the early 'bourgeoisie' had begun to cultivate a 'private' sphere of independence within the family, but had initially lacked the means to express that independence beyond the family. Around 1700, however, those means became available through the proliferation of print and the creation of new spaces for socializing.

Gradually, the once private sphere of the bourgeois family extended outwards into a 'public sphere', occupying spaces independent of the church, the court, and government. At first, this public sphere was 'literary' only, and was expressed in new genres of writing and an expanding readership; it became 'political' when the bourgeoisie was ready to claim a share of political power.

Though his philosophical inspiration was Kant's concept of the 'public' as the sphere of Enlightenment, Habermas took his evidence overwhelmingly from English sources, notably the early 18th-century journal *The Spectator*. Unsurprisingly, this Anglophile portrayal of the public sphere appealed to Anglophone historians. The appeal was reinforced by the nostalgic character of Habermas's argument, which contrasted early 18th-century bourgeois culture with what he saw as the debased mass culture of the later 19th and 20th centuries. The concept of the 'public sphere' gave the 18th century and the Enlightenment a fresh significance.

England was not, of course, the traditional centre of Enlightenment; and arguably its public sphere was politicized far earlier than Habermas imagined. Printed political debate was subject to very little restriction after the lapsing of the Licensing Act in 1695; and even *The Spectator* was not without a political purpose. But historians have been able to apply the concept of the 'public sphere' to many increasingly popular lines of enquiry into the social or cultural history of Enlightenment across Europe; if anything, moreover, the suggested distinction between a 'literary' and a 'political' public sphere was better adapted to developments in Continental Europe than to the peculiar circumstances of Britain.

After 1989, therefore, the public sphere quickly established itself as the lens through which historians view and assess the Enlightenment's impact on the societies in which it was active. Whether the institutions which historians have associated with the public sphere were also effective vehicles of Enlightenment has not, however, always been evident.

Institutions of sociability

Crucial to the emergence of a public sphere independent of government and court were new institutions of sociability. Higher levels of disposable income among the upper, and especially the middling, ranks of society created new opportunities for voluntary sociability; both men and women from these classes could afford to go out to meet friends and acquaintances, and to converse without causing scandal or giving the appearance of political intrigue. For obvious reasons these institutions were urban; rural sociability was typically limited to church or to visits to neighbours' houses. But the town or city was not simply a location; it was a resource, with the public amenities, publishing houses and booksellers, and physical venues, as well as the private wealth to support intellectual and cultural activity.

Of all the new institutions of sociability, the coffee house is the one most closely associated with the new public sphere. Coffee for public sale was introduced into Europe from Turkey in the mid-17th century, and the first coffee house opened in Venice in 1645. But it was in England that the coffee house first became widespread. There was a coffee house in Oxford in 1650, and they were soon common in London. Paris followed, with some 280 coffee houses by 1720, 600 by 1750, and 900 by 1789. Over the 18th century, they spread across the entire European Continent.

Here was a new space for socializing, one less raucous and less liable to disorder than the tavern, and which quickly developed its own self-conscious etiquette. The value of 'politeness' was transposed from its original courtly setting, where respect for hierarchy was always primary, and reframed as a requirement for orderly conversation among coffee house customers. Such conversation was assumed to be based on reading, and the genre of journals pioneered by *The Spectator* was ideally suited to the milieu: of a length and in a style to be read as contributions to conversation. Articles were intended to be entertaining, avoiding partisanship in religion or politics, but still addressing questions of general concern to coffee house readers, from fashion to country pursuits (always an urban fascination), to new public phenomena such as the growth of public credit (Figure 10).

Coffee houses and their analogues—chocolate houses may have had slightly more prestige—quickly became literary subjects in their own right, as did the stimulants they sold. Coffee in particular was associated with *esprit*, quickness of mind: the article 'Caffés'

The Coffee-house Politicians.

10. 'The Coffee-house Politicians'. A caricature of a London coffee house (1772), reflecting its reputation as a centre of political news and discussion.

in the *Encyclopédie* would depict cafés as 'manufactories of mind'. Men of letters colonized individual coffee houses, while the qualities of coffee and of chocolate were made subjects of learned enquiry. But those who wrote on them needed to do so in forms appropriate to the milieu in which they were consumed, ready to meet satire with wit. Coffee houses not only provided a market for a new style of journalism: they taught philosophers to write in ways that would enable them to reach a wider public than their peers.

A second institution which some historians have been keen to associate with the emergence of a new public sphere, and with the propagation of Enlightenment ideas, was the Masonic Lodge. Freemasonry's origins were in fraternities of stonemasons, and it retained its association with the craft through its idealization of the building of the Temple in Jerusalem, celebrating its master-builder, Hiram, and its rebuilder on return from the Jews' exile in Babylon, Zerubbabel. The movement's ostensible ambition was no less than to rebuild the Tower of Babel, restoring harmony to the world.

The first Lodge of a new kind, with a broader and higher-ranking membership, was founded in Scotland in 1599. The idea spread south to England in the 17th century, the first London Lodge being founded in 1670; but it was in the 18th century that Freemasonry took off as an institutional movement, Lodges being founded the length and breadth of the Continent. By 1800 there were 900 Lodges in France alone, with perhaps 40,000–50,000 members; there were thousands more Lodges in Europe as a whole. Lodges differed in various ways—by the 'rite' they followed, and by social composition; the apparently egalitarian character of membership belied a high level of noble participation in many Lodges. But the rapidity of Freemasonry's growth and the extent of its spread were impressive testimony to the new freedom of Europe's better-off to associate on a voluntary basis, without prompting or inhibition from above (Figure 11).

Assemblée de Francs-Maçons pour la Réception des Maîtres.
Entrée du Recipiendaire dans la Loge.

11. Freemasons. A depiction of a French Lodge whose members are about to receive new 'Master masons'. Note the paraphernalia of Masonic ritual, and the exclusively male membership.

There is nevertheless an obvious difficulty in associating Freemasonry with the public sphere: the secrecy it imposed upon its members. Its secrecy made it suspicious to rulers unaccustomed to independent, voluntary gatherings among their subjects; the Papacy, moreover, suspected Freemasons of heresy, if not of unbelief. (In fact, as its Biblical inspirations make clear, it was not antithetical to Christianity, but it excluded Jews and Muslims.) These suspicions prompted occasional attempts to suppress the movement, notably in Italian states in the middle decades of the century; later in the century fuel was added to the suspicion by the 'Illuminati', a radical variant of Freemasonry originating in Bavaria but which spread south into Italy.

For the most part, however, Freemasonry functioned more as a members-only organization, exclusive in the sense that existing members controlled the admission of new ones. An advantage of membership was the mutual recognition which lodges afforded each other, and the multi-directional correspondence which ensued. Members who travelled could call upon the Lodges in the places they visited for support: membership offered a kind of passport.

Many philosophers were members—but not all: Voltaire, Mandeville, and Hume ridiculed the movement. Freemasons, Mandeville observed, attend their Lodges and pretend their mysteries, but as far as he could see they have nothing more to do there than to be Freemasons. The sceptical historian might add that it is difficult to see what intellectual purposes could be served by membership: it is not obvious how Freemasonry could have been either an inspiration or a conduit for the arguments about religion and society described in previous chapters.

A third institution associated with the public sphere, and long regarded as the *acme* of Enlightenment sociability, was the *salon*. *Salons* flourished in Paris in the mid-18th century, attracting many of the leading men of letters in the city. They were directed by an elite of well-born or well-to-do *salonnières*, including Mme Geoffrin, Julie de L'Espinasse, Mme Helvétius, wife of the *philosophe*, and Mme Necker, wife of the Swiss banker, Jacques Necker. A strong case has been made by Dena Goodman for the intellectual agency of these women, as inspiring and directing the conversation of the men of letters whom they invited to participate, and whose friends (and sometimes lovers) they became. The *salons*, Goodman argued, constituted a public sphere in which women played a prominent and intellectually significant role.

The case seems to have been exaggerated: Antoine Lilti has demonstrated that the *salonnières'* freedom of initiative was limited by social protocol, and has emphasized just how wedded the *salons* remained to an aristocratic culture of *mondanité*, allied to a persistent commitment to status. Men of letters participated in *salons* because they offered prospects of patronage and accorded them higher social status by association; but the *salon* was not a culture they were able to shape to their own ends, intellectual or political. In fact, literary *salons* were originally a 17th- rather than an 18th-century institution: and if anything, the intellectual initiative of women was more respected in the former, thanks to the Cartesian proposition that 'the mind has no sex'. By contrast, the 18th-century *salonnières* were more deferential, dependent socially on the aristocracy and intellectually on the men of letters. The *salon* was after all neither an institution of the public sphere nor a major instrument of Enlightenment (Figure 12).

If the Paris *salons* were not the setting for female intellectual initiative some have assumed, it is now clear that London offered a more favourable context. There the group known as the 'Bluestockings' achieved recognition in their own right. Led by Elizabeth Montagu (1720–1800), whose criticism of Shakespeare earned the grudging respect of Samuel Johnson,

12. The salon. 'Le Thé à l'Anglaise, Salon of the Four Mirrors, Palace of the Temple' (1766) by Michel-Barthélemy Ollivier (1714–84). The salon is taking place in a strikingly beautiful, high-ceilinged room.

the group included Catherine Macaulay the historian, the writers Elizabeth Carter and Anna Letitia Barbauld, and the artist Angelica Kauffmann.

Radical religious 'Dissent' provided another social context supportive of women's intellectual ambitions: Mary Wollstonecraft (1759–97) and the novelist Mary Hays both moved in Unitarian and liberal Presbyterian circles in London. But such freedom was harder to sustain elsewhere, in France, Germany, and Spain. Individuals were able to take initiatives, particularly to promote the cause of female education; but only after the Revolution, in the 1790s, was there a new social space for women's intellectual and political activity in France.

In any case, it is arguable that the expanded opportunities for writers, female as well as male, owed more to the expansion of print culture than to the new institutions of sociability. For all the popularity of these institutions, it was the efforts of publishers and printers that created and sustained the public sphere.

Print culture

The 18th century saw no major innovation either in the technology of printing or in the organization of publishing, but the scale and sophistication of publishing enterprises were transformed. To take the measure of these developments, several historians have spoken of a publishing 'revolution'. This may exaggerate the extent of structural change: in the main centres publishing was increasingly separate from printing, but the industry remained flexible, and the division of labour between printing, publishing, and bookselling was by no means clear-cut. What is undeniable is the expansion of production, as the volume of books published increased across the century (Figure 13).

Existing lines continued to grow: Bibles, sermons, devotional works, and almanacs were all published in greater numbers. But

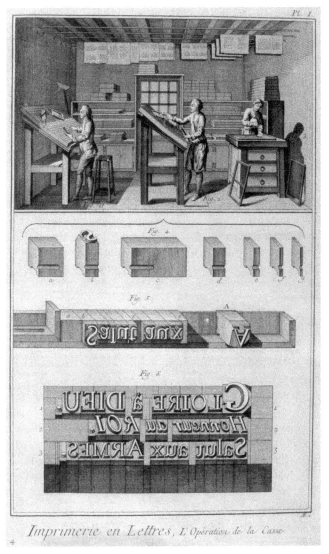

Imprimerie en Lettres, L'Opération de la Casse.

13. The printing house. Typesetting in a printing house, from volumes of plates published with the *Encyclopédie* (1762–72).

the proportion of religious works within the total published fell quite markedly: in Germany, and probably also France, from just under 40 per cent in 1740 to some 25 per cent by 1770, and 14 per cent by 1800. Growth in volume but proportional decline was also the pattern for books in Latin. The increases which explain this pattern were in periodicals, novels, histories, and scandal—the last three being forms of 'narrative' which appealed to a lay readership of men and women keen to diversify their reading.

There was also more variety, as publishers took on treatises of philosophy or political economy. Even if these were never likely to sell as well as histories, their publishers were occasionally rewarded: Adam Smith's *Wealth of Nations* was a bestseller in 18th-century terms. University textbooks, likewise now increasingly in the vernacular, also sold in growing numbers. The key here was the choice of format: while a history or a treatise of philosophy or political economy was likely to be published initially in quarto, a progressive reduction in size to octavo or even duodecimo would reduce the publisher's costs and the price to the buyer. The first two editions of the *Wealth of Nations* were published in London by William Strahan and Thomas Cadell in quarto, with a likely print run of 750 copies, and cost two guineas bound; but the third edition was an octavo, printed in 1,000 copies, selling at one guinea bound.

Historically, publishers had protected their investments by securing various forms of exclusive privilege. In France, for example, publishers' book guilds in Paris and other major cities were granted such privileges by the crown's Office of the Book Trade. In Britain the statutory introduction in 1710 of legal copyright (for fourteen years, renewable for another fourteen if the author were still alive), upheld on appeal by the House of Lords in 1774, served something of the same purpose, although shifting the original property in a work to its author. But such legal protection was effective only in relatively large, coherent jurisdictions; where the unit of jurisdiction was small, as in much of Germany, it was much less easy to enforce. Even in mainland Britain, publishers protected their business by more or less formal arrangements with others—and still found themselves powerless to prevent their books being reprinted without compensation by publishers in Dublin and in the North American colonies. An octavo edition of the *Wealth of Nations* was published in Dublin within a few months of the first quarto edition appearing in London, competitively priced at less than £1 bound. Strahan and Cadell were irate, but hardly impoverished; their own octavo edition would restore their position within the United Kingdom. Meanwhile the work itself was that much more widely available.

The most remarkable Enlightenment publishing enterprise of all was the *Encyclopédie* of D'Alembert and Diderot. The original publisher, André François Le Breton, was responsible for the first edition of seventeen volumes of text and a further eleven of plates, all published in folio between 1751 and 1772. Although expensive to produce, and interrupted in 1757 by a crisis in the censorship regime, the venture was still rewarding: by the time Le Breton sold the rights to future editions in 1768, he had made some 2.5 million livres gross profit.

But the real hero of the *Encyclopédie*'s publishing, as Robert Darnton demonstrated, was Charles-Joseph Pancoucke, who bought the rights from Le Breton. Having brought out a second folio edition between 1771 and 1776, Pancoucke obtained, on the accession of Louis XVI, a twelve-year 'privilege' which enabled him and his co-publishers, the Société Typographique de Neuchâtel, to import their new editions into France without paying customs or being subject to censorship. He used this to bargain with and ultimately to trump his rivals. First he cut a deal with Joseph Duplain, who had seen the opportunity for a quarto edition: published in Geneva and Neuchâtel between 1777 and 1779, this yielded a profit of 120 per cent on outlay. Then Pancoucke outmanoeuvred the publishers of an octavo edition in

Lausanne and Berne between 1778 and 1782, forcing them to pay him off in copies which he promptly 'dumped' on the market.

Pancoucke was handsomely rewarded for all this cut-throat enterprise, but it also benefitted readers: by 1789, there may have been as many as 14,000–16,000 copies of the *Encyclopédie* in France. The availability of the quarto and octavo editions brought it within range of purchase by men of letters themselves, and more generally by the provincial middling classes, magistrates, bourgeois, and clergy. It seems to have sold well across France, and is likely to have sold best where there were institutions, Parlements, and provincial academies, which supported intellectual life.

Those who had a clear, established interest in controlling the production and distribution of printed matter were of course the authorities, ecclesiastical and civil. In the Roman Catholic world, the Church maintained its Index of Prohibited Books. Protestant churches relied on the civil magistrate to maintain appropriate controls, and remained clear that there were lines which should not be crossed, beginning with denial of the doctrine of the Trinity, outlawed in both the United Provinces and England in the 17th century. Everywhere, moreover, the civil authorities assumed that oversight of the book trade extended to the content of books: this was an industry whose economic regulation went hand-in-hand with censorship.

The closeness of the connection, however, was also its undoing: the industry was too successful for strict controls to be maintained. No government gave way to quite the extent of the English: once the Licensing Act had lapsed in 1695, the libel laws were the chief constraint on a free press, and while these could be bent to partisan political ends, they had very little effect on intellectual life. In France, by contrast, the Director of the Book Trade employed around a hundred readers to check books before publication—yet the inadequacy of such an apparatus was clear by 1750. The Director between 1750 and 1763, Malesherbes, responded with a new flexibility. It was he who granted a 'privilege' to the first volumes of the *Encyclopédie*, and later introduced the concept of 'tacit permission', which without giving formal approval protected authors and publishers from subsequent action. A range of Enlightenment publications, including works of philosophy and political economy as well as the later volumes of the *Encyclopédie*, were the beneficiaries.

In Germany controls in the many small states could be more or less oppressive, but the variation ensured that authors could find a publisher; crucially, Frederick II's Prussia was relatively liberal. Even the Index bowed to the pressure. Faced with a 'flood' of new works, and in particular with the phenomenon of the novel, a major reform was announced in 1753 by Prospero Lambertini, Pope Benedict XIV, who en route to the top had served the Holy Office and the Index as a reader of suspect books. There was no question of abandoning the Index (something that did not happen until the late 20th century), but the strategy was now one of encouraging self-censorship by authors, and of guiding the reading of the faithful.

If censorship was no longer sustainable on a general basis, inconsistencies nevertheless continued to frustrate authors and publishers. In France the Director of the Book Trade worked alongside the police, who were responsible to the Parlement of Paris: institutional rivalry was the inevitable outcome. It was the Parlement which forced the revocation of the privilege granted to the *Encyclopédie* in 1757, halting its publication for several years, and which enforced bans on works by Helvétius and Rousseau. In Italy the implementation of the Index, which outside Rome had no officials of its own, may have been increasingly difficult; but the Church never gave up, and authors and publishers depended on rulers who often still had reason to compromise with Rome. The fate of Giannone, kidnapped and held hostage by the Dukes of Savoy while the Church proscribed his *Civil History of Naples* and confiscated the manuscript of his 'Triregno', was an enduring lesson; such explicit criticism of the Church was not heard again in the Kingdom of Naples until the 1780s. Outside of the United Kingdom and the United Provinces, the publication of works following an Enlightenment agenda still required authorial nerve and publishers' initiative.

A growing market for books presupposed increasing numbers of literate readers. Although the estimates are rough, historians believe that in France the literacy rate among men increased between 1686–90 and 1786–90 from just above a quarter to just under half, and among women from about 14 per cent to over a quarter. In England, the rates by the end of the 18th century were higher, at 60 per cent and 40 per cent respectively; in Scotland they were higher still, reaching 65 per cent among men. Such aggregate figures, however, hide many variations, among the most important the markedly higher rates of urban literacy. For Enlightenment authors and their publishers, moreover, the quality of literacy was even more important: here both the churches and the state played constructive parts. All the churches, Roman Catholic included, eased their suspicions of lay reading, while governments looked to schooling and to universities to provide them with literate and numerate officials as well as practitioners of the traditional professions of law and medicine.

Literacy not only enabled men and women to read the works of philosophers and novelists; it also inspired them to respond—to answer back. How and what readers read has attracted increasing interest among historians and literary scholars, keen to give readers agency as well as authors, and to point out that a text could escape the intention of its author.

One particularly fine study of the literature devoted to food and drink in 18th-century Paris, by Emma Spary, has demonstrated that the authority of those with apparently 'scientific' credentials was repeatedly challenged by lesser writers who refused to accept what the experts claimed. As Voltaire, Buffon, and others found, food and drink, coffee no less than spirits, were matters of taste as well as philosophy: what counted as 'enlightened' in culinary matters was constantly contested. Here as elsewhere, Rousseau's intervention against the proliferation of needs, his condemnation of luxury as indulgence, struck a particular chord, and turned readers into respondents as no one else could.

The Enlightenment author

A burgeoning print culture thus provided writers with an ever-increasing range of publishing options, and with readers confident of their ability to respond. But the print culture of the 18th century did at least as much for the standing and independent agency of authors. For several reasons, authorship has recently been devalued in intellectual and literary history. Many scholars have focused on the study of texts by themselves or in relation to other texts—'intertextuality'—uninhibited by an obligation to defer to their authors' supposed intentions. Others have put the emphasis on readers, valuing their understandings of a work above that of its author. Others still, cultural and print historians, have concentrated on books as material objects, and on their publishing and distribution. Yet it is clear that authorship mattered to writers, and various developments within print culture gave authors a new status, independence, and, literally, authority.

Most obvious among these was a greater willingness to name the author on the title page. Along with the name might be marks of status—the letters of an author's degrees, or the initials of the societies or academies of which he was a member. Where an author was rich enough, or a publisher sufficiently confident of his profits, an engraved portrait of the author might provide a frontispiece. Of course there were still circumstances in which anonymity was preferable: when a new author was uncertain of his reception, where he might attract the attention of censors, where she feared exposure. But there were other ways of identifying an author than by naming him or her on the title page: by name or by allusion in prefatory material, or by reference to previous works ('by the author of'). All affirmed the status of the author to the reader.

Another way in which author and publisher could shape the reader's perception of an author's *oeuvre* was by choice of format. As we have seen, this was an economic decision; but it also affirmed status. In his magnificent study of publishing in the Scottish Enlightenment, Richard Sher has shown how Hume responded to the frustration of the poor sales and limited impact of the *Treatise of Human Nature* and his early *Essays* by persuading his Edinburgh and London publishers to repackage his two philosophical *Enquiries* and separate volumes of *Essays* as the *Essays and Treatises on Several Subjects*, issued in a cheap, four-volume duodecimo in 1753. This was the first edition of his works to sell in appreciable numbers—one measure of recognition. But it needed to be complemented by another: publication of the *Essays and Treatises* as a single quarto volume in 1758, the quarto embodying and projecting the intellectual respect which Hume expected his philosophy and political economy to command.

Invisible to the reader, but still more important to the author, were the pecuniary rewards of publishing. Again, Sher has shown just how much authors stood to gain by negotiation with their publishers. The most successful Scots were the historians Hume and Robertson. Both employed their author's copyright to advantage. Hume sold the rights to a single edition for a fixed sum, giving him the freedom to change publishers, as he did between the first and the second volumes of the *History of Great Britain* (1754, 1757) (Figure 14). In total, from this and the *History of England* (1762) (which incorporated the *History of Great Britain*), Hume's income was more than £4,000, and possibly more than £5,000.

THE

H I S T O R Y

OF

GREAT BRITAIN.

VOL. I.

CONTAINING

The Reigns of JAMES I. AND CHARLES I.

By DAVID HUME, Esq;

EDINBURGH:

Printed by HAMILTON, BALFOUR, and NEILL.

M,DCC,LIV.

14. David Hume's *History of Great Britain*. Title page of volume 1,
covering the reigns of James I and Charles I. Published in Edinburgh
by Hamilton, Balfour, and Neill (1754). For later volumes of the
History, Hume switched to the London-Scottish publishers William
Strahan and Thomas Cadell.

Following in Hume's slipstream, Robertson did even better, selling Strahan and Cadell the copyrights for each of his histories in advance, accepting the lower sum of £600 for the first, the *History of Scotland* (1759), but then receiving more than £1,000 for each quarto volume of the subsequent *History of Charles V* (1769) and *History of America* (1777). His total earnings, Sher calculates, amounted to the equivalent of £700,000 today, making Robertson the highest-paid of all Scottish Enlightenment authors.

But historians were not the only beneficiaries. Adam Smith did not do so badly from political economy. Initially he adopted the different strategy of sharing the profits of the work with Strahan and Cadell, only later selling them the copyright (twice over, for two fourteen-year periods). Between publication of the *Wealth of Nations* in 1776 and his death in 1790, Smith had probably earned between £1,500 and £1,800 from the work. French authors also earned well from their writings. The prolific Voltaire earned most; but when the more modest Rousseau observed that the 6,000 livres he earned from *Émile* would cover his living expenses for four years, it seems that he was allowing himself a higher income than a university professor.

Authors valued their earnings for more than an enhanced standard of living. Crucially, they also brought 'independence'. To an 18th-century man of letters this meant freedom from dependence on an individual patron, from the status of a retainer. An author would most completely achieve independence when he earned sufficient to live by his writing alone: such was the position for which Hume strove all his adult life, and finally achieved in the 1760s, through the success of his *History*. Rousseau too achieved such independence, even if there were periods in which he had to earn by copying music. It was a supreme irony that the Enlightenment's two most independent authors should have had its most notorious quarrel, when Rousseau accused Hume of conspiring against him after bringing him over to England in

1766. Rousseau, who understood the connection between his independence and his celebrity, cultivated the grievance in public; Hume, who thought independence spoke for itself, was baffled (at least until he remembered that Rousseau was a Christian).

The great majority of Enlightenment authors, meanwhile, were satisfied with an independence which enabled them to combine writing with membership of a profession, as a university teacher, a doctor or a lawyer. Holding a government office was also compatible with 'independence', since whether it was held as a species of property (as under the French system of 'venality' or sale of office), or by appointment, it too accorded status without rendering its holder a direct 'dependent' of a more powerful individual.

Even those employed as tutors could negotiate in a way impossible a century before. Thus Adam Smith, who in 1764 resigned his professorship at the University of Glasgow to become tutor to the young Duke of Buccleuch on his grand tour, negotiated not only a salary of £500 but an annual pension of £300 for life, on which after two years he would return home to Kirkcaldy to write the *Wealth of Nations*. After its publication, Smith accepted a well-paid government post as a Commissioner of Customs in Edinburgh, while he prepared new editions of both his books, and was consulted as an independent adviser on economic policy by government ministers. Many others, in France, Germany, Italy and Spain, followed careers which were variations on this pattern. For these men of letters, authorship and independence were mutually reinforcing—they gave 'authority', the confidence to advance arguments on matters of public interest, and to expect the public to heed them.

Authors in the 18th century could take advantage of several recent innovations in the literary world to reinforce their status. One was the review journal, an innovation of the late 17th century, which transformed access to new developments in the world of books.

The great pioneers of the genre were Pierre Bayle, in the *Nouvelles de la république des lettres* (1684–7), Jean Le Clerc, in the *Bibliothèque universelle* (1686–93) and its successors, and Johann and Friedrich Mencke, father and son, editors (from 1682) of the *Acta eruditorum* of Leipzig. These journals not only summarized new books, often with lengthy quotations; in the hands of a Bayle or a Le Clerc, the review was an instrument of controversy, an opportunity to take the argument further. Published in cheap duodecimo, the journals informed members of the republic of letters of the arguments of books they might never have the means to acquire or the time to read; at the same time they affirmed the status of authorship.

These pioneers had many national successors, one of the earliest being the *Giornale de' letterati d'Italia*. First conceived in 1675, the *Giornale de' letterati* went through several iterations, and was successively published in Rome, Parma, Modena, and Venice before it finally ceased in 1740; it was succeeded within a few years by the Florentine *Novelle letterarie*. As well as reviews, the *Giornale* carried literary news from all the main Italian cultural centres. In England the field was headed by the *Critical* and *Monthly Reviews*; in Scotland William Robertson and others launched the first *Edinburgh Review* in 1755. Only two numbers were published (only in name was it the ancestor of the more famous early 19th-century *Edinburgh Review*), but the second, in 1756, contained Adam Smith's review of Rousseau's *Discourse on Inequality*, urging readers to recognize its importance.

Another device for the promotion of authorship was the prize essay. The most famous winner of a prize essay contest was Rousseau, for his answer to the question posed by the Academy of Dijon in 1750: 'Whether the restoration of the sciences and arts has contributed to the purification of morals?' the subject of his 'First Discourse'. Rousseau was also the best-known loser, his 'Second Discourse' failing to win the same Academy's competition in 1754, when the question concerned the origin of inequality.

Winning helped to make Rousseau's reputation; losing left him the author of perhaps the single most important, certainly the most challenging, work of the entire Enlightenment.

But among essay competitions, the one with the most enduring significance was that offered annually by the Royal Academy of Arts and Sciences in Berlin. The competitions were the initiative of Maupertuis, the *philosophe* appointed Perpetual President by Frederick II and charged with the Academy's refoundation. In spite of Frederick's Francophile agenda, however, the Academy's essay competitions proved to be a major stimulus to German scholarly and philosophical culture. Two of the most original essays were written in answer to questions on the origin of language, by J. D. Michaelis in 1759 and J. G. Herder in 1771; these not only helped to make the reputation of their authors, they brought a debate hitherto dominated by English and French authors to their German counterparts. In 1763 the question was the certainty of mathematics compared with metaphysics: the winner was Moses Mendelssohn, the runner-up Immanuel Kant.

Together, formal, government-sponsored academies and less formal, voluntary literary and debating societies were the institutions which more than any other secured the reputation and authority of men of letters. (With a few exceptions, women were excluded from these institutions, denying them the opportunities they afforded.) Whether conceived as extensions of government, like the Berlin Academy, or as independent, self-governing bodies, like the Select Society of Edinburgh, academies and societies embodied the (male) literary public sphere perhaps better than any other institution, even the coffee house. They did so because they gave men of letters status, responsibility, and a greater or lesser scope for intellectual initiative. Frederick II may have installed Maupertuis as President of the Berlin Academy, but the hard work was done by the Academy's secretary, the Berlin Huguenot Samuel Formey, his deputy, the Swiss Jean Bernard Merian, and by ordinary members such as the Swiss-German mathematician Leonard Euler, and the Swiss J. G. Sulzer, another student of language.

By contrast, the Select Society of Edinburgh was entirely independent, being the brainchild of the painter Allan Ramsay. Founded in 1754, the Select Society had among its first members the principal *literati* of Edinburgh, including Hume, Robertson, and Smith, along with a few of their friends among the landed and legal elite. There were agreed rules for the setting of questions for discussion, which were to avoid revealed religion and Jacobitism; the minutes show that the questions chosen were broadly concerned with social and economic 'improvement'.

Here the danger lay in an absence of authority to control membership. There was a clamour to join, and the membership of the Society rose to over one hundred by the end of the decade. Hume feared that so large a membership would undermine its purpose as an institution led by men of letters, and indeed it lasted fewer than ten years. But the Select Society symbolized the authority claimed by the men of letters who constituted the Scottish Enlightenment, and inspired other similar improving institutional initiatives, in Edinburgh and elsewhere in Scotland (Figure 15).

Some academies were too well established, or too closely connected with a royal or princely court, to be amenable to such a degree of direction by men of letters. An example of too close a connection was the Academy of Sciences founded by the ruler of Savoy, Victor Amadeus III, in Turin in 1783, with the clear purpose of enabling the regime to harness scientific expertise.

Among the already well established were the several royal academies in Paris, the Académie Française, the Académie des Inscriptions, and the Académie des Sciences, and the many more academies in the French provinces. Like the *salons*, their longer histories, stretching back into the 17th century, meant that both the Parisian and the provincial academies were by now well

15. 'His Majesty's Historiographer'. William Robertson, by John Kay (1790). Man of letters, historian, Moderator of the General Assembly of the Church of Scotland, Principal of Edinburgh University, founder-member of the Select Society of Edinburgh, Robertson epitomizes the intellectual seriousness and social urbanity of the Scottish Enlightenment.

integrated into the social structures of the *ancien régime*. Even so, the gradual admission of *philosophes* into the Parisian academies recognized their prominence in intellectual and literary life. Elevation to the status of *académiciens* might compromise the *philosophes'* independence, as the Grub Street journalists of Paris claimed; but it was also an acknowledgement of the status they had acquired by their writings. Out in the provinces, moreover, the academies gradually adapted to an improving agenda, promoting the union of the arts and sciences and encouraging agricultural innovation.

Enlightenment, government, and the public

A few individual *philosophes* famously gained direct, personal access to Europe's most 'enlightened' rulers: Voltaire and D'Alembert to Frederick II, Diderot to Catherine the Great. Voltaire spent three years at Potsdam, where Frederick failed to treat him with all the respect he thought his due, while Diderot made the rather longer journey to St Petersburg, there to entertain the Empress with his conversation, and, perhaps, to advise her on policy towards the nobility. At a lower level in the regal hierarchy, the Neapolitan court of Ferdinando IV and his more intelligent Habsburg wife, Maria Carolina, briefly encouraged the economist Ferdinando Galiani to think he might be useful after his enforced return from his diplomatic post in Paris, where his quick wit had made him a favourite in the *salons*. In these and other cases, however, it is clear that the philosopher's role was as much to amuse and flatter the ruler as to give advice on political and social problems sometimes remote from their experience (literally so, in the case of Diderot in Russia).

Far more important, if we wish to gauge the relation between Enlightenment and government, was the education of government ministers and officials. Such education was both formal, at universities, and continuing, through the journals, manuals, and treatises which they read as adults. The best example of a university system dedicated to the preparation of an official, governing class was that in the Protestant north of Germany. The key innovations were made in Prussia, at the new University of Halle. There the presence of a strong Pietist impulse within Lutheranism stimulated a complex series of intellectual reactions, the most fertile being the stand-off between the Pufendorfian version of natural law taught by Christian Thomasius, and the more metaphysical approach of Christian Wolff. Unsurprisingly, it was the Thomasian programme of civil philosophy, inculcating tolerance and sociable behaviour under an absolute sovereign, which was favoured by the crown as preparation for government service. In East Prussia, the university in Königsberg served a similar function.

Outwith Prussia, the key university became that of Göttingen in Hanover; the circumstance that the ruler of Hanover was also King of Great Britain distanced Göttingen from local pressures, and enabled it to attract students from all over Germany and the German-speaking world, from Catholic Bavaria to Protestant (but remote) Transylvania. It was Göttingen professors who took the initiative in transforming cameralism, the German version of 'reason of state', into the more modern *Staatswissenschaften* (state sciences); they were also the leading exponents in Germany of the new forms of stadial and universal history. Once they had left university, students who had become government officials could keep themselves up to date on intellectual and technical matters by reading a range of sophisticated journals, headed by the *Göttingische Anzeigen von gelehrten Sachen* (*The Göttingen Journal of Learned Affairs*), founded 1739, or the *Zeitung des Hamburgischen unpartheyischen Correspondenten* (*The Hamburg Impartial Correspondent*), founded in 1730.

Another university system to undergo radical reform in the first half of the 18th century was the Scottish, as first Glasgow, then Edinburgh and the Aberdeen colleges, and finally St Andrews abandoned the system of generalist teaching by 'regents' or tutors, and instituted chairs in specific disciplines. Increasingly these were held by the leading figures of the Scottish Enlightenment, among whom only Hume never held a university position. Within the United Kingdom these universities were educating young men for the professions rather than central government, which, being concentrated in London, continued to recruit from an unreformed Oxford and Cambridge. But Scottish-educated professionals not only provided day-to-day administration within Scotland; they were to be found holding office in disproportionate numbers in British North America and in the British East India Company.

Less open to reform were the universities and colleges of Italy and the Iberian peninsula. Yet even here there were initiatives in specific areas. In Lombardy, Beccaria followed the publication of his work *On Crimes and Punishments* (1764) by lecturing on political economy, and subsequently served as an official of the Austrian government, as did the economist Pietro Verri. At the University of Naples a new chair in Commerce and Technology was created for Antonio Genovesi in 1754 by his friend, the Tuscan agricultural administrator, Bartolomeo Intieri. Having hitherto held chairs in theology and philosophy, Genovesi self-consciously set himself to teach the more modern, useful science of political economy to the 'studious youth' of the kingdom.

Political economy also became part of the education of Spanish and Portuguese administrators, both those who remained at home and those sent out to the Americas. Inspired by the Italian Muratori's ideal of 'public happiness', Gerónimo de Uztáriz, Antonio de Ulloa, and Pedro de Campomanes placed economics at the heart of the Spanish monarchy's policymaking. Still more important for the empire, by the later 18th century creoles (Spanish colonial citizens born in the Americas), such as the future Argentine general Manuel Belgrano, were able to receive their education in Spain (in civil law), and return to senior administrative positions in the colonies, in Belgrano's case as Secretary of the *Consulado* or maritime tribunal in Buenos Aires. Between Portugal and its major colony, Brazil, there was only one institution of higher education, at Coimbra in Portugal; but this was reformed by Pombal in 1772 with the specific purpose of adapting it to the education of imperial administrators. In the Americas too, formal education was subsequently kept up to date by a vigorous local culture of literary and scientific journals, such as the *Gazeta de Leteratura de México* (1788–95).

The political contribution of those who championed an Enlightenment intellectual agenda was not limited to the education of the governing class. More radically, the Enlightenment's adherents would also transform expectations of the relation between philosophers and men of letters and those in power. Not satisfied with the traditional, humanistic role of counsellors to princes, they now put themselves forwards as spokesmen for the 'public', the formers of 'public opinion'. Nor was this simply aspiration; there was a definite sense of entitlement. As authors, as philosophers who had made such strides in understanding the 'progress of society', exponents of Enlightenment were confident that they possessed the intellectual authority to direct the public's opinion.

The premise was a growing conviction that 'opinion' was the key to modern politics. Hume put his finger on the point in one of his earliest essays, 'Of the first principles of government' (1741):

> Nothing appears more surprizing to those, who consider human affairs with a philosophical eye, than the easiness with which the many are governed by the few; and the implicit submission, with which men resign their own sentiments and passions to those of their rulers. When we enquire by what means this is effected, we shall find, that, as force is always on the side of the governed, the governors have nothing to support them but opinion. It is therefore on opinion only that government is founded; and this maxim extends to the most despotic and most military governments, as well as to the most free and most popular.

In another early essay, Hume was sanguine about the consequences of the 'liberty of the press' for which England was famous—and if his fear of the unrestrained growth of public debt later made him much more critical of this liberty, the problem remained one of managing opinion.

A critical view of English 'liberty' and of the excessive, destabilizing power of 'opinion' in British politics was widespread in France, where exponents of absolute monarchy strove to maintain the old orthodoxy: that affairs of state, and especially the royal finances, were a 'reason of state', not to be rendered public. But as tensions within *ancien régime* society proliferated and spilled over into print, a traditional posture of denial became unsustainable: 'opinion' existed, and had to be managed.

As we saw in Chapter 3, the economists of the Gournay circle were among the first to see the point, publishing a whole range of economic writings the better to inform public debate on commercial and financial policy. Later the Swiss banker Jacques Necker went still further, publishing a 'Compte rendu' of the monarchy's finances in 1781; it sold in tens of thousands of copies. By then more radical thinkers, including Raynal and Louis-Sébastien Mercier, were characterizing public opinion as a 'tribunal', and turning it explicitly against royal authority. By 1780, the contest for 'public opinion' was at the heart of French politics.

Arguably the most radical exponents of public opinion as a new politics, however, were the Neapolitans. Antonio Genovesi led the way with his appeal to the 'studious youth' of the kingdom to assume its moral and economic leadership, promoting the public good without waiting for the monarchy. But the fullest development of the idea came from the leader of the next generation of Neapolitan Enlightenment reformers, Gaetano Filangieri (1752–88), author of the *Scienza della legislazione* (1780–5). Radicalizing Montesquieu's argument that legislation should be the means of change, Filangieri would have all laws derive from the 'tribunal' of public opinion. Public opinion, in turn, would rest on a secure foundation only if it had to plead its case in a free press. A free press alone would ensure that sovereignty lay 'constantly and really in the people'. Rulers should therefore govern by the 'suffrage' of public opinion, as the expression of the people's will.

The point of this appeal to public opinion was not that it actually existed in the form Filangieri imagined—least of all in the

Kingdom of Naples. It was the potential of public opinion as a political force which the philosophers projected, and which they expected to shape. Here too their thinking had a distinctive intellectual foundation. Enlightenment philosophers did not cast themselves as the philosopher-kings of Plato's imagination, determining what was just and applying it to their communities. Rather, Hume, Gournay, and Filangieri appealed to public opinion precisely because they understood the constraints which a modern economy and society now placed on political action. A commercial economy was one in which a multitude of individuals took decisions about what to sell and what to buy, decisions far too numerous to be effectively regulated by government. When Adam Smith appealed to governments to refrain from intervention in the market, it was not simply or even chiefly because he feared the ambitions of the state; it was also because he knew that most such intervention was futile. Governments simply did not have the capacity to do what traditional 'reason of state' had supposed they should; and the best hope of restraining government ambition was to empower 'public opinion', as informed and directed by philosophers.

This not to say that there was nothing for governments to reform. Commerce still faced major obstacles, and the greatest of these, as Hume, Smith, and Filangieri agreed, was the survival of the 'feudal system' on the land, and the relations of personal dependence which it entailed. The dismantling of this system should be the priority of modern government, from Scotland to Naples; and along with legislation, it would require the education of public opinion in favour of agricultural improvement.

In Scotland the opportunity for just such a programme arose after the defeat of the last Jacobite rebellion in 1745; in the second half of the century the Scottish Highlands were made a laboratory for experiments in agronomy, town planning, and environmental change. Over the same period, the agriculture of the Scottish Lowlands was transformed even more dramatically, great landlords such as Adam Smith's pupil, the Duke of Buccleuch, turning themselves into highly successful agrarian capitalists. Showing the way were a succession of agricultural and improving societies, beginning in 1723 with Society of Improvers in the Knowledge of Agriculture, and continuing in 1750s with the Society for the Encouragement of the Arts, Sciences and Manufactures, a subsidiary of the Select Society, and the Gordon's Mill Farming Club, an offshoot of the Aberdeen Philosophical Society.

Such societies made explicit the commitment to bettering the human condition on earth. Over the second half of the 18th century they spread widely in Europe. The first in Spain was the Real Sociedad Bascongada de los Amigos del País (the Royal Basque Society of Friends of the Nation), founded by leading families in the Basque towns of Azcoitia and Bergara in 1765; between 1770 and 1820, seventy more such societies were founded in peninsular Spain, and a further fourteen in Spanish America. In Habsburg Bohemia, nobility, academics, and government officials combined in 1770 to found the Society of Ploughing and the Free Arts, renamed the Patriotic Agricultural Society in the 1780s.

Where the monarchy was still nervous of independent initiatives among its subjects, as in Naples, small groups of reformers met informally in provincial cities to discuss ways and means of improving their localities. Giuseppe Maria Galanti in Foggia, Melchiorre Delfico in Teramo, and Giuseppe Palmieri in Lecce, all combined writing on agricultural conditions with galvanizing sympathetic members of the local elites. Followers of Genovesi and contemporaries of Filangieri, such men sought to enlarge the scope for voluntary, extra-governmental agency. They exemplified what Enlightenment philosophers had in mind when they looked to 'public opinion' to persuade governments to carry out necessary reforms—and to recognize that a modern, commercial society was not theirs to regulate and exploit just as they wished: a modern government was one aware of its own limitations, willing to try its actions at the bar of informed public opinion, and to accept its verdict.

Enlightenment and revolution

For many historians, the last question to be asked of the Enlightenment remains the most important of all: what was its relation to revolution? The question can be asked of the American Revolution of 1776–88; and most American historians would now accept some connection. But the question is most obviously pressing in the case of the revolution which began in France in 1789 and culminated in the *coup d'état* by Napoleon in 1799, and which in the course of the 1790s inspired or instigated further revolutions across Europe, from the Netherlands to Naples. A revolution as aggressively and violently ideological as the French, so most historians would reason, must have owed something to the Enlightenment.

There is no denying that there were continuities between Enlightenment and revolution—continuities of men, women, and ideas. Among the younger generation of *philosophes* who committed themselves to the Revolution, the most famous was the Marquis de Condorcet (1743–94), mathematician, social scientist, and historical philosopher, whose *Esquisse d'un tableau historique des progrès de l'esprit humain* (translated as *The Sketch*) was published posthumously in 1797.

Another to combine historical philosophy with revolutionary commitment was Francesco Mario Pagano, author of the *Political Essays*; having drafted the constitution of the short-lived Neapolitan Republic of 1799, Pagano was executed in the reaction which followed the restoration of the Bourbons by Admiral Nelson. Another 'martyr' of the Neapolitan Republic was the expatriate Portuguese noblewoman, Eleonora Fonseca Pimentel, editor of the revolutionaries' newspaper.

Mary Wollstonecraft also made no secret of her sympathies, although she did not have to die for the cause. Shortly after publishing *A Vindication of the Rights of Women* in 1792 she visited Paris to observe the revolution at first hand.

Continuities at the level of ideas were exemplified by the revolutionaries' constant invocation of the work of Montesquieu and Rousseau: the single most important work of revolutionary political thought, the Abbé Sièyes' *Qu'est-ce que le tiers état?* (*What is the Third Estate?*) (1789), was written in dialogue with both. To these sources of inspiration revolutionaries added new ones from the later Enlightenment, most famously the concepts of the rights of man and woman. Political economy too was a revolutionary as much as an Enlightenment preoccupation, as successive revolutionary regimes struggled to manage the national debt whose failure had brought down the monarchy.

Continuities, however, do not make the Revolution the outcome of the Enlightenment. The contrary is just as arguable. On the account of the Enlightenment's politics offered in this book, the Revolution was the antithesis of Enlightenment. Where Enlightenment philosophers looked to an informed public opinion to exert an indirect, restraining influence on government, the revolutionaries were committed to the overthrow of the *ancien régime* by direct action. Revolution, in other words, was the revenge of political agency upon the impersonal, gradual process of change envisaged by the Enlightenment concept of the 'progress of society'. Thinking of revolution in this way is by no means incompatible with supposing that books were among its causes. But the books which mattered are just as likely to have been the semi-pornographic novels which purported to expose the sexual and moral corruption of the court as the treatises of philosophers. In Robert Darnton's influential view, it was works such as *Thérèse philosophe* and the *Anecdotes sur Mme du Barry*, coupled with the aggressive journalism of ill-paid, radicalized younger authors, which did most damage to the credibility of the French monarchy;

what they alleged was then spread with devastating effect as rumour on the street.

Some historians have sought to maintain a distinction between the early phases of revolution, which can be identified with the ideals of Enlightenment, and the Terror, which abandoned them. But such attempts to match ideas so precisely to action quickly break down. The French Revolution was an unanticipated and never-before-experienced political process which swept up and transformed those who participated in it. Typically young, few of its leaders, in France and beyond, had had time to be intellectually or politically prominent before 1789. Those of an older generation who committed themselves to it, like Condorcet or Pagano, did so by personal choice; others whose writings had been no less critical of the *ancien régime*, like Pagano's fellow-reformer Galanti, chose not to commit themselves, and stood aside.

By its end, early in the 19th century, certain intellectual preoccupations remained, to be sure, but the political context and the political agenda had been transformed. The philosophers' confidence that bad or arbitrary government might be contained and re-educated by creating an informed public opinion had been blown away: the key questions facing modern politics had become those of democracy—what were its social foundations, how far did popular sovereignty extend, how was it to be represented? Finding answers to these questions which were compatible with the ever-quickening pace of economic transformation would preoccupy conservative, liberal, and socialist thinkers alike throughout the 19th century and beyond. They were not the questions which had engaged the attention of the Enlightenment.

It is true that several initiatives characteristic of the Enlightenment were resumed and carried forward after the French Revolution. One such was the agricultural improving society, which became ubiquitous across Europe, from Hungary and southern Italy to

Ireland, and spread extensively in Spanish America. Enlightenment thinking about landownership, in particular the desirability of eliminating 'servile' relations of tenancy, also informed policymaking in Europe and its overseas empires: it has been argued, for example, that the land reforms effected by the British in India early in the 19th century owed much to the arguments of the Scottish economists.

But the renewal of identifiably Enlightenment initiatives does not make them continuous with their 18th-century forerunners. For they were resumed in a world whose political framework had been transformed by the French Revolution and its aftermath. Henceforth the influence of the Enlightenment cannot be dissociated from the outcomes of the Revolution. Unsurprisingly, contemporaries, particularly those hostile to the Revolution and its consequences, were unable to distinguish the two: the anti-*philosophes* traced the origins of the Revolution to the triumph of philosophy over religion and social hierarchy in the decades before 1789, and alleged that the Revolution itself was a philosophers' conspiracy. The later, 19th- and 20th-century critique of Enlightenment, however, is another story, briefly to be considered in Chapter 5. The Enlightenment with which this book has been chiefly concerned—the 18th-century movement of intellectual enquiry and self-conscious engagement with 'the public'—was over.

Chapter 5
The Enlightenment in philosophy and history

By the second decade of the 21st century, it has become common for historians of the Enlightenment to explain to their readers 'why it still matters'. Most historians assume that the past has some bearing on the present, and believe that the subject of their work matters. But they don't usually feel the need to tell their readers quite so explicitly; in doing so, recent historians of Enlightenment have been an exception.

By contrast, this book represents a step back from such an approach, to concentrate on historical reconstruction of the Enlightenment. I have sought to portray Enlightenment thinking and Enlightenment thinkers in terms appropriate to their time, in the 18th century. If this has meant acknowledging that Enlightenment philosophers and historians engaged with ideas and arguments of 17th-century predecessors, it is also intended to capture their originality—what was new in their thinking, and in their conception of the public role of the philosopher. But I am less inclined to insist on the Enlightenment's continuing relevance to our own time.

It cannot be denied, even so, that the legacy of the Enlightenment has been contested ever since the 18th century: modern historians anxious to tell their readers 'why it still matters' are responding to what they believe to be continued attempts to denigrate or even reverse the Enlightenment's achievements. Complicating the picture, moreover, has been the presence of philosophers alongside historians in the debate.

Increasingly, it seems that contesting the Enlightenment's legacy has become an argument between the disciplines, with historians defending the 'modernity' of the Enlightenment against the philosophers' 'postmodern' critiques. The implication is that philosophers have been criticizing a phenomenon whose history they do not understand, and whose continued relevance to the present they have accordingly misrepresented. The account of the Enlightenment offered in this book, however, suggests that this may not be fair to the philosophers. As we saw in the opening chapter, *lumières*, *Aufklärung*, and Enlightenment were philosophers' concepts before they were taken up and reconstructed by historians. In this concluding chapter, accordingly, I want to revisit the philosophers' Enlightenment, the better to understand why the Enlightenment's legacy has become so contested.

The philosophers' Enlightenment

The original identification of 'Enlightenment' with 'philosophy' did not mean that Enlightenment was bound to one set of philosophic principles. D'Alembert's insistence that all knowledge must be understood to derive from the senses and Kant's critical philosophy were radically different. In moral philosophy similarly large differences separated the natural law of Thomasius from the accounts of the moral sentiments offered by Hume and by Smith, and again from the rational voluntarism of Kant's universally applicable 'categorical imperative'.

Nor was 'philosophy' understood in exclusively intellectual terms. The anti-*philosophes* were right to identify their enemies, the *philosophes*, as much by their style of thinking and conception of their role as by their philosophical principles. Whatever their philosophy, those who identified with the *parti des philosophes* were also committed to the diffusion of knowledge to the public, and to its use to the benefit of mankind. Nevertheless, the attacks of the anti-*philosophes*, before and after the Revolution, would serve to consolidate the identification of Enlightenment with philosophy.

In the long run, however, the anti-*philosophes* mistook their target: it was not the philosophy of the *Encyclopédie* which would be identified with Enlightenment, but that of Kant. Thanks not least to his own assiduous efforts to promote it in German universities, while simultaneously encouraging others to write histories of philosophy which excluded the alternatives, Kant's philosophy gained a dominant position in German-reading Europe. As a result, his reassertion of the primacy of reason in human understanding and insistence on the necessity of a universal basis for moral judgement were accepted as the essential philosophical principles of the Enlightenment. By definition, therefore, to criticize Kantian philosophy was to criticize the Enlightenment.

The first to make this association, early in the 19th century, was Hegel; his followers, the idealists, carried the baton into the second half of the century and beyond. Discounting its historical dimension, the Hegelians held that Kantian, Enlightenment philosophy had been abstract and static, unable to grasp the forward movement of history. Possessing only an etiolated concept of progress, it had failed to integrate its ideas with the great economic, social, and political transformations which, beginning in the 18th century, came to a head in the 19th. Only a Hegelian historicism could achieve such a synthesis, and grasp the purpose, the end, of history.

It was in the 20th century, however, that critique of the Enlightenment as philosophy began in earnest. Now the charge was not that Enlightenment philosophy was insufficiently historicist, but that it had overreached itself. In its ambition to reorder knowledge for the benefit of mankind, it had created new instruments of domination, both technological and political, which the debased culture of the masses under capitalism was incapable of resisting. This was the argument of the most famous, if also the most difficult, of the critiques of Enlightenment, Theodor Adorno and Max Horkheimer's *Dialectic of Enlightenment*, first published in German in 1944. The authors were social philosophers, founders of the Frankfurt School in wartime exile in America. Emphasizing the continuities between classical Greek and Enlightenment thinking, they argued that the Enlightenment had failed to overcome the contradictions of liberalism, and was thus implicated in the very developments to which it should have been opposed: fascism and even anti-Semitism.

After World War II, additional strands were added to the critique. One was provided by the German historian, Reinhart Koselleck, in *Critique and Crisis* (first published in 1959). Indebted to the pre-war legal philosopher Carl Schmitt's analysis of the Hobbesian sovereign state, Koselleck's critique focused on the inadequacy of the Enlightenment's response to absolute monarchy. By pursuing moral philosophy in isolation from politics, and taking the secretive rites of Freemasonry as their model of sociability, Koselleck argued, the Enlightenment's adherents had undermined the authority of the state which was the necessary condition of civil peace.

At much the same time, Isaiah Berlin began to question the adequacy of Enlightenment rationalism and universalism by constructing a 'Counter-Enlightenment', whose chief proponents, Vico and Herder, were portrayed as advocates of moral and cultural pluralism. Although Berlin thought of himself as a historian of ideas, his Counter-Enlightenment was deliberately abstracted from historical context: his target was a philosophical outlook, identified with the Enlightenment, which too confidently proclaimed the truth of our knowledge and the universality of our values.

The critique intensified in the 1970s and 1980s, as a prominent feature of the intellectual and cultural movement known as 'postmodernism'. Postmodernism was hardly a uniform movement—and indeed made no virtue of uniformity; its critique of Enlightenment was no exception. Among its earliest and most influential exponents was the French philosopher Michel Foucault. In *The Order of Things* (first published in 1966, translated in 1970), Foucault struck at the root of the assumption that human nature was a stable starting point for the Enlightenment's moral, social, and economic enquiries, arguing that 'man' emerged as a subject in the 18th century only as a result of an arbitrary shift at the 'archaeological' level of thought; no credit for the new focus could be attributed to Enlightenment thinkers. Subsequently, in *Discipline and Punish* (1975), Foucault renewed Adorno and Horkheimer's charge of the Enlightenment's hidden authoritarianism, finding it at the heart of 18th-century thinking about crime and punishment.

English-speaking philosophers soon joined in. In *After Virtue* (1981), the Catholic, once also Marxist philosopher, Alasdair MacIntyre, claimed to have identified a specific 'Enlightenment project', aimed at providing an independent rational justification of morality. MacIntyre believed that the project was illusory; morality requires a metaphysical foundation, and of those historically available, he argued, Thomism remains the most cogent. By contrast, metaphysics, let alone religious conviction, was completely absent from Richard Rorty's critique of the supposition that knowledge or morals has a foundation we can call true. In *Philosophy and the Mirror of Nature* (1979), Rorty deconstructed the claim that the mind reflects or represents nature, and can thus establish truth. Radicalizing Wittgenstein, Rorty argued that all we can do is use language to describe what is out there, and to prescribe moral rules to ourselves. There may be many such languages: we have to choose between them and follow our convictions. The Enlightenment's, in particular Kant's, confidence that it had identified a universal, rational formula for true knowledge and morals was mistaken.

The cumulative force of this tradition of philosophic critique of the Enlightenment is almost certainly the stronger for the shortage of convincing defences. The work most usually seen as offering a sympathetic account is Ernst Cassirer's *The Philosophy of the Enlightenment*, published in Germany in 1932, before Cassirer left for exile in England, Sweden, and the United States. A neo-Kantian, Cassirer understood Enlightenment philosophy to have been pre-Kantian; nevertheless, he identified the underlying principle of the Enlightenment as the 'autonomy of reason'. Given Cassirer's status as a Jewish exile from Nazism, one might expect his exposition of Enlightenment philosophy to command respect, yet it fell flat. Cassirer was generally thought to have come off second best in his famous encounter with Heidegger at Davos in 1929; despite his Nazi affiliation, it was Heidegger who would be of greater interest to later Wittgenstinians such as Rorty. Even Isaiah Berlin was critical. Reviewing the 1951 English translation of *The Philosophy of the Enlightenment*, Berlin described it as 'serenely innocent', its author unaware of the conflicts and subversive forces which had later overwhelmed Enlightenment philosophy.

The historians' response

It was in the absence of a convincing philosophical defence of the Enlightenment that historians took up its cause after World War II. They may have done so because, after the horrors of the 20th century, the Enlightenment of the 18th century represented Europe's better past; but as historians they also had methodological commitments of their own, about which they were typically less explicit than the philosophers. In the 1950s and 1960s, many historians of the European Enlightenment subscribed to a version of modernization theory, be it Weberian or Marxist. They identified Enlightenment with the twin forces of secularization and economic development, and generally assumed that it was 'modern' in its thinking and its political orientation.

The tendency for historians to identify Enlightenment with 'modernity' became even more marked after 1989. Three circumstances explain this. The first was the fall of the Berlin Wall, and the concomitant crumbling of Marxism's credentials as a methodological framework for progressive, leftist thinking. The second was the revival of religion as a force in politics, and an explicit challenge to secular values. And the third was postmodernism, with what many historians regarded as its impudent relativization of truth.

In response to these developments, historians took inspiration from Habermas's nostalgic portrayal of the 18th-century 'public sphere' (conveniently translated into English in 1989). In conception, in the 1960s, Habermas's work had been a fresh contribution to the Frankfurt School's critique of modern mass culture as a product of late capitalism; but in its debt to Kant's idea of the 'public' it was also implicitly sympathetic to Enlightenment as an earlier, better model of modernity. This made it congenial to historians in the 1990s, who welcomed a characterization of Enlightenment which was post-Marxist but 'modern', and also consistent with recent trends in research into the Enlightenment as a social as well as intellectual movement.

After 2000, the equation of Enlightenment with 'Modernity' became almost axiomatic among historians (and the capital 'M' increasingly common), and many were explicit in their desire to refute the postmodern philosophic critique. None was more aggressive in these respects than Jonathan Israel, who turned from economic to intellectual history in the course of writing a comprehensive history of the early modern Netherlands.

In a succession of volumes, beginning with *Radical Enlightenment: Philosophy and the Making of Modernity 1650–1750* (2001), Israel not only proclaimed the Enlightenment's secularism; unusually for a historian, he associated it with a specific philosophy, claiming that true, 'radical' Enlightenment was necessarily based on the monist metaphysics of Spinoza. Without exception, it seemed, the 18th-century arguments for the 'modern' values of tolerance, democracy, human rights, and gender equality had depended on a specific, materialist philosophical system. Not since the heyday of classical Marxism had a historian been so confident in challenging philosophers on their own ground.

If without the same degree of hubris, Anthony Pagden's conviction that the Enlightenment 'still matters' rests on a similar equation of Enlightenment with 'the modern world': and he too is ready to take on the philosophers, MacIntyre in particular. Some historians, it is true, have objected that 'modernity' is too exclusively associated with the West; but the solution, to extend it globally, in one case all the way to 19th-century China and Japan, simply stretches still further the historians' claim that the concept is theirs to define and to distribute.

The Enlightenment in historical perspective

The willingness of historians to stand up for the Enlightenment has been a salutary counterweight to the persistent criticism of the philosophers. But it is by no means clear that historians have always understood the philosophers' critique, or the implications of their own espousal of 'modernity'. For one thing, the critique has been less one-sided than historians suppose. In 1983, a year before his death, Foucault revisited the question 'What is Enlightenment?' It was the question from which modern philosophy was unable to escape, since Enlightenment, Foucault conceded, is the 'attitude' characteristic of 'modernity'. But the Enlightenment was also 'an event', 'or a set of events and complex historical processes, that is located at a certain point in the development of European societies'. As such, he now argued, it should not be treated as identical with the recurrence of the 'humanist' concept of man. It was still necessary to renounce the Enlightenment's encompassing rationalism; but Foucault believed that this left Kant's idea of critique intact, if it was understood as the individual will to challenge authority. This might be Enlightenment construed as Kantian anarchism, but it offered a scope for agency, for action in time, which Foucault had once seemed to deny.

A late essay by Rorty on 'The continuity between Enlightenment and postmodernism' (2001) was similarly conciliatory. The critique of foundationalism in philosophy was not so much 'postmodern' as a continuation of the Enlightenment's own critique of the foundational role of God in human affairs. In any case, to dispense with Enlightenment rationalism carries no adverse implications for Enlightenment politics: the goals of diminishing cruelty and enhancing liberty remain valid, even if it is now clear that they cannot be implemented as quickly or as comprehensively as rationalist (Kantian) utopians suppose.

Meanwhile other philosophers, not associated with postmodernism, have been stating the case for Enlightenment in terms which respond to the arguments of its critics. For all Habermas's debt to Kant for his concept of the 'public sphere', his substitution of 'communicative reason' for 'subject-centred reason', as Rorty pointed out, represents a significant shift towards those who hold that morality is constructed within language. North American Kantians too have compromised, in Chicago if not in Harvard, by envisaging the possibility of a 'non-foundational' Kantianism. From this perspective, Samuel Fleischacker has interpreted Kant's question 'What is Enlightenment?' as an invitation to critical public discussion in which diversity of opinion will flourish.

Non-Kantians have also begun to contribute to the philosophers' debate. Genevieve Lloyd makes the obvious point that many Enlightenment thinkers, from Diderot to Adam Smith, were more interested in the powers of the imagination than in those of reason; to this she adds, following Arendt, that even Kant's vision of world citizenship required the imagination to 'go visiting'. More subtly, she suggests that what is most challenging in the philosophy of Kant is its orientation to the future: shifting the metaphor, she argues that we should think of Enlightenment not as a light which, once revealed, should never be covered, but instead as a moment of illumination which cast shadows forwards from the 18th century. By standing in those shadows, we enable ourselves to review what that future has become.

There is therefore more to the philosophers' debate over Enlightenment that the historians' one-sided affirmation of its 'modernity' has allowed. It is not within this book's—or this author's—compass to try to effect a *rapprochement* between the two ways of approaching Enlightenment. But there is certainly scope for a greater degree of mutual respect. More philosophers might recognize that there was more to the Enlightenment than Kant; historians that the concept of 'modernity' cannot be exclusively identified with liberal values and human well-being, but has long been treated by philosophers as ambiguous and contested.

Beyond this, what an intellectual-historical approach to the Enlightenment—the approach taken in this book—may offer is historical perspective. I have argued that 'philosophy' was already present in the 18th-century concepts of *lumières* and *Aufklärung*; almost everywhere, in France and in Germany, in Scotland and in Italy, it featured prominently among the interests and in the writings of Enlightenment authors. If it is hardly surprising that later philosophers should have retained an interest in interpreting the Enlightenment's legacy, however, this does not mean that we can assume continuity between them. The languages or discourses of philosophy in the 18th century were different, and they have since been adapted and transformed in ways which a history focused upon the Enlightenment cannot easily contain.

Equally, we have seen that the idea of the 'modern' interested 18th-century thinkers. They thought of themselves as 'moderns' as opposed to 'ancients', and they asked why modern Europe was different from and in important respects more developed than antiquity. Extrapolating from this, they further asked why the modern European world had progressed so much further, was so much more 'civilized', than the less well-off, apparently simpler peoples Europeans had encountered in the New World.

But as most Enlightenment thinkers also realized, modern Europeans could behave just as cruelly as those supposedly less civilized peoples; worse still, the Europeans' 'progress' might be at the expense of the others' backwardness. Enlightenment thinkers already knew that to be 'modern' was to be compromised. They might be convinced that material betterment for all in this world was a goal worth pursuing; but Rousseau's *Discourse on Inequality* would remind them that its costs, in inequality and moral compromise, would need to be recognized.

In its political economy no less than its philosophy, moreover, the Enlightenment was far removed from the early 21st century. Between the two lie the French Revolution; the rise of nationalism and the nation state in the 19th century; and in the 20th, two world wars, the Holocaust, and the fateful mid-century ideological polarization over the meaning of 'socialism'. In the meantime, the study of economics, the social sciences, and politics has been transformed no less than philosophy, and universities have established themselves in the role of arbiters of scientific discourse and, directly or indirectly, policy advice; for its part, public opinion has long escaped the tutelage of philosophers and men of letters. Modern democracies and modern autocracies face economic, social, political, and now also environmental challenges inconceivable in the 18th century.

At this distance, therefore, we should not be trying to reassure ourselves that the Enlightenment still matters. But we can enrich our own thinking, our awareness of the variety of ways of understanding human affairs, by imaginatively reconstructing the conceptual languages of Enlightenment thinkers, recognizing the problems they encountered, and appreciating the originality of their responses to them. It is not the relevance of the past which the intellectual historian seeks, but the challenge of understanding how problems were formulated, addressed, and conceptualized in terms different from those we use now.

What is particularly interesting about Enlightenment thought was its willingness to engage with change in this world independent of the next, to think about what might constitute 'progress'. Precisely because so much human catastrophe lies between it and our world in the 21st century, this commitment to progress, to human betterment, challenges our comprehension. If the Enlightenment can now only cast shadows over us, it continues to be intensely rewarding to study and understand it, and to engage with its intellectual achievements.

References

Chapter 2: Engaging with religion

David Hume, *The Natural History of Religion*, critical edition by
　　T. L. Beauchamp (Oxford, 2007), p. 35.
Voltaire, *Treatise on Toleration*, ed. Simon Harvey (Cambridge, 2000),
　　p. 25.
Edward Gibbon, *The Decline and Fall of the Roman Empire*, ed. David
　　Womersley (London, 1995) vol. 1, ch. 15, p. 447; vol. 3, ch. 50,
　　note 114, p. 192.

Chapter 3: Bettering the human condition

Adam Smith, *The Theory of Moral Sentiments*, ed. D. D. Raphael and
　　A. L. Macfie (Oxford, 1976; Indianapolis, 1984), pp. 50, 61, 184–5.
Samuel Pufendorf, *On the Duty of Man and Citizen*, ed. J. Tully
　　(Cambridge, 1991), pp. 118–19.
John Locke, *Two Treatises of Government*, ed. P. Laslett (Cambridge,
　　1960, 1988), pp. 319, 354, 315.
David Hume, *A Treatise of Human Nature*, ed. P. H. Nidditch (Oxford,
　　1978), book 3, part 3, section 5, p. 615.
David Hume, *Essays, Moral, Political, and Literary*, ed. E. F. Miller
　　(Indianapolis, 1985), pp. 629, 331, 263.
Jean-Jacques Rousseau, *The Discourses and Other Early Political
　　Writings*, transl. and ed. V. Gourevitch (Cambridge, 1997),
　　pp. 170, 187.
Adam Smith, *The Wealth of Nations*, ed. R. H. Campbell and
　　A. S. Skinner (Oxford, 1976; Indianapolis, 1982), p. 540.

Chapter 4: Enlightening the public

Hume, *Essays*, p. 32.

Gaetano Filangieri, *Scienza della legislazione*, ed. V. Ferrone, A. Trampus, et al. (Venice, 2003–4). For 'public opinion', book 1, ch. 7.

Chapter 5: The Enlightenment in philosophy and history

Isaiah Berlin, 'Review of Cassirer, *The Philosophy of the Enlightenment*', *English Historical Review*, 68 (1953).

Michel Foucault, 'What is Enlightenment?' (1983), *The Foucault Reader*, ed. Paul Rabinow (London, 1991), p. 43.

Further reading

General introductions

An excellent introduction, up to date in its references but with an argument of its own, is Dan Edelstein, *The Enlightenment: A Genealogy* (Chicago, 2010). A good general survey is Dorinda Outram, *The Enlightenment* (Cambridge, 3rd edition, 2013). Fuller, interpretative, and strong in intellectual history, is Anthony Pagden, *The Enlightenment and Why It Still Matters* (Oxford, 2013).

The most discussed recent interpretation of the Enlightenment is that of Jonathan Israel, in four large volumes: *Radical Enlightenment: Philosophy and the Making of Modernity 1650-1750* (Oxford, 2001), *Enlightenment Contested: Philosophy, Modernity and the Emancipation of Man 1670-1752* (Oxford, 2005), *Democratic Enlightenment: Philosophy, Revolution and Human Rights 1750-1790* (Oxford, 2011), and *Revolutionary Ideas: An Intellectual History of the French Revolution from the Rights of Man to Robespierre* (Princeton, 2014).

Works of reference include J. W. Yolton, with R. Porter, P. Rogers, and B. M. Stafford (eds), *The Blackwell Companion to the Enlightenment* (Oxford, 1991); and, in four volumes, A. C. Kors (ed.), *Encyclopedia of the Enlightenment* (Oxford, 2001).

Noteworthy recent publications in other languages include: G. Paganini and E. Tortarolo (eds), *Illuminismo: un vademecum* (Turin, 2008), a series of twenty short essays on themes in Enlightenment thought, and S. Van Damme, *À toutes voiles vers la*

vérité. Une autre histoire de la philosophie au temps des Lumières
(Paris, 2014).

Enlightenment texts

The complete text of the *Encyclopédie, ou dictionnaire raisonnée des sciences, des arts et des metiers* (1751–72) is available free from the University of Chicago's ARTFL Encyclopédie Project, edited by Robert Morrissey and Glenn Roe: <http://portail.atilf.fr/encyclopedie/ Formulaire-de-recherche.htm>. It reproduces the first, Paris edition and provides summary data as well as the capability to search the text. There is an English translation by Richard Schwab of D'Alembert's *Preliminary Discourse to the Encyclopédie* (Chicago, 1995).

Several paperback series offer accessible editions and translations of the Enlightenment texts mentioned in this book. These include:

Cambridge Texts in the History of Political Thought (Cambridge University Press): Beccaria, Condorcet, Diderot, Ferguson, Hobbes, Hume, Kant, Locke, Montesquieu, Pufendorf, Rousseau, Vico.

Cambridge Texts in the History of Philosophy (Cambridge University Press): Condillac, Herder, Kant, Shaftesbury, Smith, Voltaire.

The Liberty Press (Liberty Fund, Indianapolis): Bayle, Carmichael, Grotius, Hutcheson, Hume (*Essays, History*), Locke, Mandeville, Smith.

Oxford University Press publishes several editions of Hume's philosophical works and a World's Classics edition of his *Essays*. It also publishes critical editions of the works of Hobbes and Locke.

For Gibbon, see *The Decline and Fall of the Roman Empire* (1776–88), in the edition in three volumes edited by David Womersley (London: Penguin, 1995).

Chapter 1: The Enlightenment

On the 18th-century uses of *lumières*: Roland Mortier, *Clartés et Ombres du Siècle des Lumières: Études sur le XVIIIe siècle littéraire* (Geneva, 1969); on the German debate over *Aufklärung*, James

Schmidt (ed.), *What is Enlightenment? Eighteenth-Century Answers and Twentieth-Century Questions* (Berkeley and London, 1996), which contains the essays by Mendelssohn and Kant in answer to the question 'Was ist Aufklärung?'

On the *Querelle* of the ancients and moderns: Dan Edelstein, *The Enlightenment: A Genealogy*, esp. chs 3, 5, 6.

On the Scientific Revolution: Lawrence M. Principe, *The Scientific Revolution: A Very Short Introduction* (Oxford, 2011), although the author disowns the term.

More generally on the history of philosophy in the 17th and 18th centuries: M. Ayers and D. Garber (eds), *The Cambridge History of Seventeenth-Century Philosophy*, 2 vols (Cambridge, 2003); K. Haakonssen (ed.), *The Cambridge History of Eighteenth-Century Philosophy*, 2 vols (Cambridge, 2006).

On the anti-philosophes: Darrin M. McMahon, *Enemies of the Enlightenment. The French Counter-Enlightenment and the Making of Modernity* (Oxford and New York, 2001).

Historical reconstruction of the Enlightenment: the key early works by literary scholars are Paul Hazard, *The European Mind 1680–1715* (first published in French in 1935; English translation London, 1953), and Daniel Mornet, *Les origines intellectuelles de la Révolution française 1715–1787* (Paris, 1933). Franco Venturi's early work included *Jeunesse de Diderot (1713–1753)* (Paris, 1939).

On the geographical expansion of Enlightenment: Roy Porter and Mikulas Teich (eds), *The Enlightenment in National Context* (Cambridge, 1981). A crucial contribution to its social history was Robert Darnton, 'The high Enlightenment and the low life of literature in pre-Revolutionary France', *Past and Present*, 51 (1971), reprinted in *The Literary Underground of the Old Regime* (Cambridge, MA, 1982). The study of women in the Enlightenment now starts from Sarah Knott and Barbara Taylor (eds), *Women, Gender and Enlightenment* (Basingstoke, 2005). On the proliferation of Enlightenment 'languages', John Pocock, 'Historiography and Enlightenment: a view of their history', *Modern Intellectual History*, 5 (2008).

Chapter 2: Engaging with religion

Jonathan Israel's case for identifying radical, irreligious Enlightenment as the true Enlightenment is best stated in *Radical Enlightenment* (2001), the first of his four volumes listed under 'General introductions'. For the alternative case: H. R. Trevor-Roper, 'The religious origins of the Enlightenment', in his *Religion, the Reformation and Social Change* (London, 1967).

On 17th-century developments in the study of religion, natural and sacred: Dmitri Levitin, *Ancient Wisdom in the Age of the New Science: Histories of Philosophy in England c. 1640–1700* (Cambridge, 2015).

On the late 17th and early 18th century critics of religion, anticipating Israel: Margaret Jacob, *The Radical Enlightenment: Pantheists, Freemasons and Republicans* (London, 1981); and Ira O. Wade, *The Clandestine Organization and Diffusion of Philosophic Ideas in France from 1700 to 1750* (Princeton and London, 1938). Curious about rather than critical of religion: Lynn Hunt, Margaret Jacob, and Wijnand Mijnhart, *The Book that Changed Europe: Picart & Bernard's Religious Ceremonies of the World* (Cambridge, MA, and London, 2010).

On 18th-century Biblical studies: Jonathan Sheehan, *The Enlightenment Bible: Translation, Scholarship, Culture* (Princeton and Oxford, 2005). See also: Adam Sutcliffe, *Judaism and Enlightenment* (Cambridge, 2003).

On the arguments over toleration: O. P. Grell and R. Porter (eds), *Toleration in Enlightenment Europe* (Cambridge, 2000); J. Parkin and T. Stanton (eds), *Natural Law and Toleration in the Early Enlightenment* (*Proceedings of the British Academy*: 186, Oxford, 2013).

On arguments for and from the 'rights of man': Lynn Hunt, *Inventing Human Rights: A History* (New York, 2007).

On the civil and the sacred in 18th-century historiography, the rich, multi-volume study of Gibbon and his contexts by John G. A. Pocock, *Barbarism and Religion*, 6 vols: *I The Enlightenments of Edward Gibbon* (1999), *II Narratives of Civil Government* (1999), *III The First*

Decline and Fall (2003), *IV Barbarians, Savages, and Empires*
(2005), *V Religion: The First Triumph* (2010), *VI Barbarism:
Triumph in the West* (2015).

Chapter 3: Bettering the human condition

General: M. Goldie and R. Wokler (eds), *The Cambridge History of
Eighteenth-Century Political Thought* (Cambridge, 2006).

On natural law and moral philosophy, T. J. Hochstrasser, *Natural Law
Theories in the Early Enlightenment* (Cambridge, 2000); Ian Hunter,
*Rival Enlightenments: Civil and Metaphysical Philosophy in Early
Modern Germany* (Cambridge, 2001).

On historical writing: Hugh Trevor-Roper, *History and the
Enlightenment* (New Haven and London, 2010); M. S. Phillips, *Society
and Sentiment: Genres of Historical Writing in Britain 1740–1820*
(Princeton, 2000); Silvia Sebastiani, *The Scottish Enlightenment: Race,
Gender and the Limits of Progress* (Basingstoke and New York, 2013);
and Pocock's *Barbarism and Religion*, esp. *IV Barbarians, Savages and
Empires*. On Hume as philosopher and historian: James Harris, *David
Hume: An Intellectual Biography* (New York and Cambridge,
forthcoming 2016).

On the origin of languages debate: Avi Lifschitz, *Language and
Enlightenment: The Berlin Debates of the Eighteenth Century* (Oxford,
2012).

On Rousseau: R. Wokler, *Rousseau* (Oxford, 1995).

On the critique of empire: S. Muthu, *Enlightenment Against Empire*
(Princeton and Oxford, 2003).

On political economy: I. Hont, *Jealousy of Trade: International
Competition and the Nation State in Historical Perspective*
(Cambridge, MA, 2005), is now fundamental.

On Hume (both his account of sociability and his political economy) and
Genovesi: John Robertson, *The Case for the Enlightenment: Scotland
and Naples 1680–1760* (Cambridge, 2005).

On Adam Smith there is an excellent, readable intellectual biography by Nicholas Phillipson, *Adam Smith: An Enlightened Life* (London, 2010).

Chapter 4: Enlightening the public

For the concept of the 'public sphere': Jürgen Habermas, *The Structural Transformation of the Public Sphere: An Enquiry into a Category of Bourgeois Society* (Oxford, 1989; translation of the German original, published in 1962).

Good general historical treatments are: James Van Horn Melton, *The Rise of the Public in Enlightenment Europe* (Cambridge, 2001); and Thomas Munck, *The Enlightenment: A Comparative Social History 1721–1794* (London, 2000).

On coffee and other alimentary issues: E. C. Spary, *Eating the Enlightenment: Food and the Sciences in Paris, 1670–1760* (Chicago and London, 2012).

On Freemasonry: Margaret Jacob, *Living the Enlightenment: Freemasonry and Politics in Eighteenth-Century Europe* (Oxford, 1991).

On the salons: Dena Goodman, *The Republic of Letters: A Cultural History of the French Enlightenment* (Ithaca and London, 1994), answered by Antoine Lilti, *The World of the Salons: Sociability and Worldliness in Eighteenth-Century Paris* (Oxford and New York, 2015; abridged translation of the French original of 2005).

On academies: Daniel Roche, *Le siècle des lumières en province: Académies et académiciens provinciaux 1680–1789*, 2 vols (Paris, 1978), and Jeremy Caradonna, *The Enlightenment in Practice: Academic Prize Contests and Intellectual Culture in France, 1670–1794* (Ithaca, 2012); for the Berlin Academy, Lifschitz, *Language and Enlightenment*.

On publishing the *Encyclopedia*, the brilliant article by Robert Darnton, 'The *Encyclopédie* wars of pre-revolutionary France', *American Historical Review*, 78 (1973).

On the Scots, their London publishers, and much more: Richard B. Sher, *The Enlightenment and the Book: Scottish Authors and their Publishers in Eighteenth-Century Britain, Ireland and America* (Chicago and London, 2006).

On Enlightenment, governments, and reform: Franco Venturi, *Utopia and Reform in the Enlightenment* (Cambridge, 1971); Derek Beales, *Joseph II*, 2 vols (Cambridge, 1987, 2009); John A. Davis, *Naples and Napoleon: Southern Italy and the European Revolutions 1780–1860* (Oxford, 2006); Paschalis M. Kitromilides, *Enlightenment and Revolution: The Making of Modern Greece* (Cambridge, MA, and London, 2013); Gabriel Paquette, *Enlightenment, Governance, and Reform in Spain and its Empire 1759–1808* (Basingstoke, 2008), and *Imperial Portugal in the Age of Atlantic Revolutions: The Luso-Brazilian world c. 1770–1850* (Cambridge, 2013).

On economic improvement, in agriculture and manufactures: Fredrik Albritton Jonsson, *Enlightenment's Frontier: The Scottish Highlands and the Origins of Environmentalism* (New Haven and London, 2013); Joel Mokyr, *The Enlightened Economy: An Economic History of Britain 1700–1850* (New Haven and London, 2012).

On Enlightenment, opinion, print, and revolution: Keith M. Baker, *Inventing the French Revolution: Essays on French Political Culture in the Eighteenth Century* (Cambridge, 1990); Robert Darnton, *The Forbidden Best-sellers of Pre-Revolutionary France* (London, 1996).

Understanding of the relation between revolutionary political thought and its Enlightenment predecessors has been transformed by the studies of Michael Sonenscher, *Before the Deluge: Public Debt, Inequality and the Intellectual Origins of the French Revolution* (Princeton and Oxford, 2007), and *Sans-culottes: An Eighteenth-Century Emblem in the French Revolution* (Princeton and Oxford, 2008).

Chapter 5: The Enlightenment in philosophy and history

Besides editing *What is Enlightenment? Eighteenth-Century Answers and Twentieth-Century Questions*, James Schmidt is the author of a series of helpful articles on the modern debate over 'Enlightenment': see, for example, 'Misunderstanding the question: "What is Enlightenment?": Venturi, Habermas, and Foucault', *History of European Ideas*, 37 (2011). See now also, Vincenzo Ferrone, *The Enlightenment.* History of an Idea (Princeton and Oxford, 2015).

The major philosophical critics have been: Theodor W. Adorno and Max Horkheimer, *Dialectic of Enlightenment* (German edition, 1944; in English, New York, 1972, London, 1997); Reinhart Koselleck, *Critique and Crisis: Enlightenment and the Pathogenesis of Modern Society* (in German, 1959; English translation, Oxford, 1988); Isaiah Berlin, *Three Critics of Enlightenment: Vico, Hamann, Herder*, ed. H. Hardy (Oxford, 2013), which includes works published from the 1960s; Michel Foucault, *The Order of Things: An Archaeology of the Human Sciences* (London, 1970); *Discipline and Punish: The Birth of the Prison* (London, 1977); *The Foucault Reader: An Introduction to Foucault's Thought*, ed. Paul Rabinow (London, 1984), which contains the lecture 'What is Enlightenment?'; Alasdair MacIntyre, *After Virtue: A Study in Moral Theory* (London, 1981); Richard Rorty, *Philosophy and the Mirror of Nature* (Thirtieth Anniversary Edition, Princeton, 2009).

For the defence: Ernst Cassirer, *The Philosophy of the Enlightenment* (Princeton, NJ, 1951); Habermas, *Structural Transformation of the Public Sphere*; K. M. Baker and P. H. Reill (eds), *What's Left of Enlightenment? A Postmodern Question* (Stanford, 2001), containing Richard Rorty's essay 'The continuity between Enlightenment and postmodernism'; Samuel Fleischacker, *What is Enlightenment?* (Abingdon and Oxford, 2013); Genevieve Lloyd, *Enlightenment Shadows* (Oxford, 2013).

For the historians Israel and Pagden, see references under Chapter 1.

For an egregious example of the global extension of 'modernity': Sebastian Conrad, 'Enlightenment in global history: a historiographical critique', *American Historical Review*, 117 (2012).

Index

Index

Index

HUMANISM
A Very Short Introduction
Stephen Law

Religion is currently gaining a much higher profile. The number of faith schools is increasingly, and religious points of view are being aired more frequently in the media. As religion's profile rises, those who reject religion, including humanists, often find themselves misunderstood, and occasionally misrepresented. Stephen Law explores how humanism uses science and reason to make sense of the world, looking at how it encourages individual moral responsibility and shows that life can have meaning without religion. Challenging some of the common misconceptions, he seeks to dispute the claims that atheism and humanism are 'faith positions' and that without God there can be no morality and our lives are left without purpose.

THE EUROPEAN UNION
A Very Short Introduction

John Pinder & Simon Usherwood

This *Very Short Introduction* explains the European Union in plain English. Fully updated for 2007 to include controversial and current topics such as the Euro currency, the EU's enlargement, and its role in ongoing world affairs, this accessible guide shows how and why the EU has developed from 1950 to the present. Covering a range of topics from the Union's early history and the ongoing interplay between 'eurosceptics' and federalists, to the single market, agriculture, and the environment, the authors examine the successes and failures of the EU, and explain the choices that lie ahead in the 21st century.

www.oup.com/vsi

FREE SPEECH
A Very Short Introduction
Nigel Warburton

'I disapprove of what you say, but I will defend to the death
your right to say it' This slogan, attributed to Voltaire, is frequently
quoted by defenders of free speech. Yet it is rare to find anyone
prepared to defend all expression in every circumstance,
especially if the views expressed incite violence. So where do
the limits lie? What is the real value of free speech? Here, Nigel
Warburton offers a concise guide to important questions facing
modern society about the value and limits of free speech:
Where should a civilized society draw the line? Should we be free
to offend other people's religion? Are there good grounds for
censoring pornography? Has the Internet changed everything?
This Very Short Introduction is a thought-provoking, accessible,
and up-to-date examination of the liberal assumption that free
speech is worth preserving at any cost.

FRENCH LITERATURE
A Very Short Introduction
John D. Lyons

The heritage of literature in the French language is rich,
varied, and extensive in time and space; appealing both to its
immediate public, readers of French, and also to aglobal
audience reached through translations and film adaptations.
French Literature: A Very Short Introduction introduces this lively
literary world by focusing on texts - epics, novels, plays, poems,
and screenplays - that concern protagonists whose adventures
and conflicts reveal shifts in literary and social practices. From
the hero of the medieval *Song of Roland* to the Caribbean
heroines of *Tituba, Black Witch of Salem* or the European
expatriate in Japan in *Fear and Trembling*, these problematic
protagonists allow us to understand what interests writers and
readers across the wide world of French.

GERMAN LITERATURE
A Very Short Introduction
Nicholas Boyle

German writers, from Luther and Goethe to Heine, Brecht, and Günter Grass, have had a profound influence on the modern world. This *Very Short Introduction* presents an engrossing tour of the course of German literature from the late Middle Ages to the present, focussing especially on the last 250 years. Emphasizing the economic and religious context of many masterpieces of German literature, it highlights how they can be interpreted as responses to social and political changes within an often violent and tragic history. The result is a new and clear perspective which illuminates the power of German literature and the German intellectual tradition, and its impact on the wider cultural world.

'Boyle has a sure touch and an obvious authority...this is a balanced and lively introduction to German literature.'

Ben Hutchinson, TLS

HUMAN RIGHTS
A Very Short Introduction
Andrew Clapham

An appeal to human rights in the face of injustice can be a heartfelt and morally justified demand for some, while for others it remains merely an empty slogan. Taking an international perspective and focusing on highly topical issues such as torture, arbitrary detention, privacy, health and discrimination, this *Very Short Introduction* will help readers to understand for themselves the controversies and complexities behind this vitally relevant issue. Looking at the philosophical justification for rights, the historical origins of human rights and how they are formed in law, Andrew Clapham explains what our human rights actually are, what they might be, and where the human rights movement is heading.

THE REFORMATION
A Very Short Introduction
Peter Marshall

The Reformation transformed Europe, and left an indelible mark on the modern world. It began as an argument about what Christians needed to do to be saved, but rapidly engulfed society in a series of fundamental changes. This *Very Short Introduction* provides a lively and up-to-date guide to the process. Peter Marshall argues that the Reformation was not a solely European phenomenon, but that varieties of faith exported from Europe transformed Christianity into a truly world religion. It explains doctrinal debates in a clear and non-technical way, but is equally concerned to demonstrate the effects the Reformation had on politics, society, art, and minorities.

www.oup.com/vsi

ROMANTICISM
A Very Short Introduction
Michael Ferber

What is Romanticism? In this *Very Short Introduction*
Michael Ferber answers this by considering who the romantics
were and looks at what they had in common – their ideas, beliefs,
commitments, and tastes. He looks at the birth and growth
of Romanticism throughout Europe and the Americas, and
examines various types of Romantic literature, music, painting,
religion, and philosophy. Focusing on topics, Ferber looks at the
rising prestige of the poet; Romanticism as a religious trend;
Romantic philosophy and science; Romantic responses to the
French Revolution; and the condition of women. Using examples
and quotations he presents a clear insight into this very diverse
movement.

SCIENTIFIC REVOLUTION
A Very Short Introduction
Lawrence M. Principe

In this *Very Short Introduction* Lawrence M. Principe explores the exciting developments in the sciences of the stars (astronomy, astrology, and cosmology), the sciences of earth (geography, geology, hydraulics, pneumatics), the sciences of matter and motion (alchemy, chemistry, kinematics, physics), the sciences of life (medicine, anatomy, biology, zoology), and much more. The story is told from the perspective of the historical characters themselves, emphasizing their background, context, reasoning, and motivations, and dispelling well-worn myths about the history of science.

www.oup.com/vsi